W9-BAN-318

101 killer apps

for your

Pocket PC

Rick Broida and **Dave Johnson**

McGraw-Hill /Osborne

New York   Chicago   San Francisco   Lisbon
London   Madrid   Mexico City   Milan   New Delhi
San Juan   Seoul   Singapore   Sydney   Toronto

The McGraw·Hill Companies

McGraw-Hill/Osborne
2100 Powell Street, 10ᵗʰ Floor
Emeryville, California 94608
U.S.A.

To arrange bulk purchase discounts for sales promotions, premiums, or fund-raisers, please contact **McGraw-Hill/Osborne** at the above address. For information on translations or book distributors outside the U.S.A., please see the International Contact Information page immediately following the index of this book.

101 Killer Apps for Your Pocket PC

1234567890 CUS CUS 01987654

Book p/n 0-07-225433-5 and CD p/n 0-07-225434-3
parts of
ISBN 0-07-225432-7

Publisher:	Brandon A. Nordin
Associate Publisher and Editor-in-Chief:	Scott Rogers
Executive Editor:	Jane K. Brownlow
Project Editor:	Emily K. Wolman
Project Manager:	LeeAnn Pickrell
Acquisitions Coordinator:	Agatha Kim
Technical Editor:	Denny Atkin
Copy Editor:	Bill McManus
Proofreader:	Susie Elkind
Indexer:	Valerie Perry
Computer Designer:	Kelly Stanton-Scott
Illustrators:	Melinda Lytle, Kathleen Edwards
Series Design:	Kelly Stanton-Scott, Peter F. Hancik

This book was composed with Corel VENTURA™ Publisher.

For Mom and Dad.

–Rick

For the two best kids on earth, Evan and Marin.

–Dave

About the Authors

Rick Broida has been a technology writer for nearly 15 years. He is the founder and former editor of *Handheld Computing Magazine* and the author of over a dozen books, including the best-selling *How to Do Everything with Your Palm Handheld* (McGraw-Hill/Osborne, 2003). Broida's writing credits include Cnet, *Computer Shopper, PC Magazine,* and *Wired.* He lives in Michigan with his wife and two children, where he authors the Tech Savvy column for Michigan's *Observer & Eccentric* newspapers. His hobbies include basketball, kickboxing, and computer gaming.

Dave Johnson is a technology journalist with nearly three dozen books to his credit. He writes *PC World*'s Digital Focus (a weekly digital photography newsletter) and is the former editor of *Mobility Magazine.* He's an award-winning wildlife photographer and the author of *The Wild Cookie,* an interactive children's story on CD-ROM. Dave is also a dedicated—but entirely talentless—guitarist, though he tries to make up for that deficiency by dressing like Pink Floyd's Roger Waters. Before Dave started writing, his somewhat unfocused career included flying satellites, driving an ice cream truck, photographing a rock band, stocking shelves at Quick Check, teaching rocket science, and writing novels about intergalactic space penguins. Today, he relaxes by photographing wolves; he's also a SCUBA instructor and underwater photographer.

Denny Atkin has been writing about technology since 1987 and about handheld computers since the Newton's release in 1993. He's worked with pioneering technology magazines as such as *Compute!, Omni,* and *Handheld Computing.* Atkin lives with his wife and son in Vermont, a state where PDAs are nearly as popular as maple syrup.

Contents

Acknowledgments

What more can be said about the superb folks at Osborne McGraw-Hill? Without Jane Brownlow, Agatha Kim, and Emily Wolman, this book would be little more than incoherent notes on a napkin. Kind thanks also to Bill McManus, Susie Elkind, and Valerie Perry. The OMH staff is, after all these many books, more than editors—they're friends, confidants, and, as is often the case, bail bonds. We also want to thank our good friend Denny Atkin, who, though he was raised by dingoes in the Australian Outback, nonetheless keeps flagging our libelously inaccurate comments.

Rick adds:

My heartfelt thanks go out not only to Dave, whose grammatically questionable prose and unique brand of "humor" make my writing look much better, but also to Shawna, Sarah, and Ethan, who have to put up with the inevitable grumpiness that comes from having too much work and too little time. Thanks for all the pop runs and "vacation Tuesdays."

Dave adds:

You can't spend a few months of your life writing a book without a great support system of friends and family. Thanks to my wife, Kristen, for keeping me sane as I wrote this book while actually making a cross-country move. And special thanks to Rick. Not only are you a great friend, but your uncanny ability to be wrong about everything and anything of any consequence whatsoever has made me look soooooo much better by comparison.

Introduction

We make no secret of our love of PDAs. They're such amazing little devices, packing more computing power than many desktop systems of yesteryear. Indeed, while most people purchase PDAs primarily for their organizational capabilities, they can do much more—much, much more. Much.

It was with that in mind that we wrote this book. It's time for you to learn just how capable your PDA really is, from helping you count calories to showing you last night's episode of *Alias*. This book is all about using your Pocket PC to do unexpected, unusual, and fun stuff. We've rounded up 101 of the best programs available for the Pocket PC and offered them up for you on a silver platter. Literally. The silver platter (otherwise known as a CD-ROM) at the back of this book is crammed with most of the programs we discuss in this book. That means you can read about a program and install it immediately—no need to locate it on the Internet and then download it (though this is the case for a few).

By the way, you might be wondering what we mean when say "Pocket PC." This book is for anyone who has a device that runs the Windows Mobile operating system (which was originally the Pocket PC operating system, hence our frequent references to the devices as "Pocket PCs"). That includes models from Compaq, Hewlett-Packard, ViewSonic, Toshiba, and other companies. No matter what kind of Pocket PC PDA you have, this book's killer applications will help you do more and have more fun.

What's Inside

This book is arranged into nine chapters, each one dedicated to a different way to use your PDA. We start you off with a bunch of great tools for getting more out of your PDA at work—Chapter 1 is filled with killer apps for your PDA that help you deliver PowerPoint presentations, manage your phone calls, carry databases, and even read Adobe Acrobat (PDF) documents. From there, we look at applications designed to make your next trip more fun and productive with city guide software, restaurant guides, language translators, and more. And that's the way the book works. In subsequent chapters, we offer diversions like e-books, wine selection, exercise, and digital music. There are chapters full of games, money managers, utilities to make your Pocket PC run better, and more. If it's a killer app, you can read about in the book, then install it from the bundled CD.

Killer Tip   *In most cases, what you'll find on the CD are trial versions of software. If you like a program and want to keep using it past its trial period, then you need to pay a small shareware registration fee to get unlimited access to the full program.*

We'd also like to draw your attention to a few special elements that we included to help you get the most out of the book:

■ **Notes**   These paragraphs include interesting stuff that will help you win the next edition of *Trivial Pursuit: Obscure Facts About Books Written by Dave and Rick Edition.*

■ **Killer Tips**   These miraculous tidbits of prose tell you how to do something smarter or faster.

■ **Sidebars**   In each chapter, you'll find a tip so great, so helpful, and so amazing that we decided to put it in its own special box.

■ **Find It on the CD**   At the end of each killer application, we give you all the cold, hard stats about the program—what the full, commercial version costs, the name of the developer, and where to find it on the Web. This is what the box looks like:

FIND IT ON THE CD
Wine Enthusiast Guide, $19.95
LandWare
www.landware.com

Installing Software on Your PDA

So, you want to be a rock star? Well, then you're reading the wrong book. But if you're ready to dig into this tome and explore all the cool programs we have to offer you, then you might want to know how to install all those apps on your device.

You can install almost any app in this book in either of two ways:

■ Grab the program from the bundled CD-ROM. The CD is organized by number, just like the programs in this book. Thus, to find a specific program, just find its number and follow the supplied links to install it on your PC or find it on the Web.

■ Find it on and download it from the Internet using the URL that we provide in the box at the end of each application description.

Which is better? It depends. The CD is faster, which is why we gave it to you to begin with. But in some cases, there might be a better, newer version of the program on the Internet, so the Web is a pretty good route as well. It's up to you.

Killer Tip *Make sure you take note of where you're saving the downloaded file! We recommend just putting it on the Windows desktop (or in your My Documents folder), as it'll be easy to find. You can simply delete it after installing the program on the PDA.*

Thankfully, installing Pocket PC software is a piece of cake. With 99 percent of the programs, there's usually an installer—a program called setup.exe or something similar—that, when double-clicked, walks you through each step of the installation process.

Killer Tip *Running out of storage space on your Pocket PC? You can install programs on a memory card instead of in main memory. During the installation process for any given program, you'll be asked if you want to install the program using the default directory. Click No, and then select the memory card from the option box that appears.*

Stay in Touch

Can't get enough of Rick or Dave? You can send questions and comments to rickbroida1@excite.com or dave@bydavejohnson.com. Thanks, and enjoy reading the book!

Chapter

On the Job

Ah, work. Is any task so sweet, any labor so gratifying? Dost anything but the fresh feeling of driving into the office inspire such poetry in our hearts?

Well, probably. Right off the top of our heads, we can think of a dozen things we'd rather do than work. On the other hand, throw your Pocket PC into the work mix and you have something else entirely. PDAs can lighten your workload and make it easier to get jobs done on the go. Most of all, using your PDA to work is just plain cool. Instead of hauling out a seven-pound laptop, imagine slipping a six-ounce Pocket PC out of your pocket—and getting essentially the same work done. In this chapter, we've found a slew of ways for you to work more efficiently by employing a PDA instead of a desktop PC, laptop, tablet, or some other nineteenth-century contraption. Dig in, and have a better day at work!

1 TextMaker

Write a Report with Complex Formatting

Until recently, claiming that you wanted to get a PDA to do some word processing on the go was little more than a joke. The Pocket PC's Pocket Word application, for instance, is badly named. Instead of delivering most of the features of Word on a handheld, it is little more than a text editor. Here's a good test: try copying a Word document from the desktop to your PDA. You'll find that documents transferred from the PC lose most of their formatting and even have their font reset to something you don't want. And forget about inserting pictures, tables, page numbering, or any other sophisticated formatting elements—Pocket Word simply does not support any of those features. The best you can hope for with Pocket Word, in fact, is simply to write something on the go and then later massively edit it once you are back on the desktop.

Not anymore. TextMaker, from a company called SoftMaker Software, is a true word processor with most of the features you'd expect to find on the desktop. It has all the goodies—fonts, bullets, tables, sections and chapters, headers and footers, you name it. Here is a look at TextMaker with some of its menus open, revealing its many features:

To make the best use of TextMaker, you should disable the file conversion that runs when you copy a Word document to your Pocket PC. Ordinarily, ActiveSync converts these files to Pocket Word format and throws away most of the formatting in the process. Since TextMaker can preserve all that fancy formatting, it's best to just disable the file conversion. To do that, follow these steps:

1. Double-click the ActiveSync icon in the System Tray so you see the Microsoft ActiveSync window:

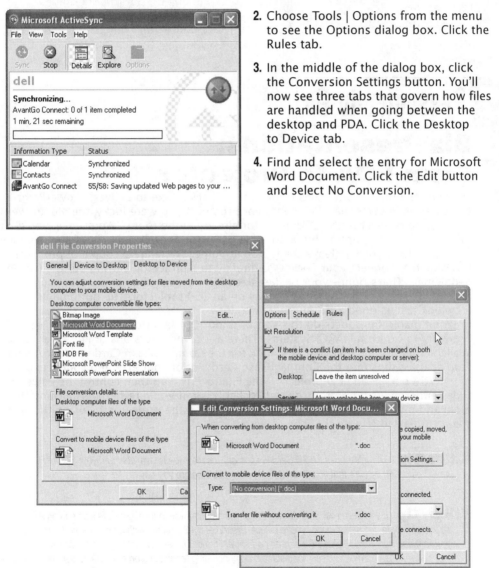

2. Choose Tools | Options from the menu to see the Options dialog box. Click the Rules tab.

3. In the middle of the dialog box, click the Conversion Settings button. You'll now see three tabs that govern how files are handled when going between the desktop and PDA. Click the Desktop to Device tab.

4. Find and select the entry for Microsoft Word Document. Click the Edit button and select No Conversion.

5. Click OK to close the various dialog boxes.

You should now be set. To test, drag a Word file from your hard disk to the My Documents folder on your Pocket PC. It should arrive unchanged. Now you can edit documents from the desktop on your PDA without losing any formatting!

FIND IT ON THE CD
TextMaker, $49.95
SoftMaker Software
www.softmaker.de

2 Presenter-to-Go

Biz Presentations: From PDA to Projector

POWER APP

You're on the road, many miles from home. What's it take to deliver a PowerPoint presentation in someone else's conference room? If you were lucky, the old answer was "a laptop to connect to the LCD projector already in the room." Worst case, you'd have to haul not just the laptop, but a portable projector as well. Talk about sore shoulders.

These days, you can leave the laptop at home. There are a couple of products available that connect your Pocket PC directly to a projector, cutting out the laptop middleman. That's right—your pocket-sized PDA is more than powerful enough to display full-resolution PowerPoint slides on an LCD projector. The bottom line is that they look just as good as if you used a laptop.

What magical products do this sort of thing? Our favorite is a gadget called Presenter-to-Go from MARGI Systems. There are several versions of Presenter-to-Go available, but for most Pocket PCs, look for the CompactFlash Card version. A small CF Card adapter slips into the CompactFlash Card slot of your PDA and connects directly to the VGA port of an LCD projector (see Figure 1-1). You then control the PowerPoint slides either by using buttons on the Pocket PC or, if you'd rather walk around the room and put some distance between yourself and the projector, by using the small, credit card-sized remote that comes with it.

Killer Tip   *Though there's an SD Card version of Presenter-to-Go available and your Pocket PC may have an SD card slot, be sure that your Pocket PC is compatible before you buy it.*

Killer Tip   *If you have ever said, "I wish there was an easy way to display a PDA's screen on a big screen so lots of people can see at once," you're in luck. Presenter-to-Go comes with a utility called MARGI Mirror. This program duplicates the Pocket PC's screen and shows it, more or less in real time, on the projector. You can use it to perform PDA training classes, for instance, demonstrating techniques on the PDA screen as the display responds to your every screen tap.*

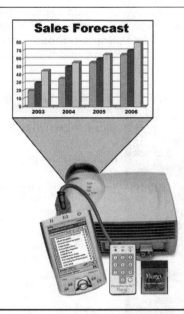

FIGURE 1-1   Presenter-to-Go attaches to your PDA and displays PowerPoint slides on a traditional LCD projector.

Getting your PowerPoint presentation into the PDA is easy. Using the software that comes with Presenter-to-Go, you can simply open your slideshow in PowerPoint, then save the file as a Pocket PC–ready file and ActiveSync to transfer it to your PDA.

And you did it all without a laptop. Is that cool, or what?

FIND IT ON THE CD

Presenter-to-Go, $199
MARGI Systems
www.margi.com

3 Pocket SlideShow

Take PowerPoint with You

Have you noticed how there's no Pocket PowerPoint program in your Pocket PC? That's disappointing, especially if you're the sort of person who reviews a lot of presentations as part of your job. Rick never leaves his basement, but Dave is often seen strutting about town, Pocket PC in hand. What's he doing? Probably thumbing through a PowerPoint presentation. How? By using Pocket SlideShow, a $20 application from CNetX.

It works pretty much the way you would expect. To get your PowerPoint slides into the Pocket PC, just drag and drop them into your PDA's My Documents folder. The slides don't come through in their original format, though—they're optimized for the Pocket PC screen. You'll see a Slide Conversion Options dialog box that lets you choose how much to shrink the files:

Which one do you choose? The 320×240-pixel mode is best for ordinary viewing, but if you have a VGA adapter for your Pocket PC, you can also use Pocket SlideShow to display the slides on a big screen. If that's in your plans, choose 640×480 or 800×600 instead.

Once the slides are on your PDA, you can view them in a dual-pane screen with the slide title and notes at the bottom of the display, like this:

Or, if you prefer, you can choose View | Slideshow from the Pocket PC's menu and view the slides full screen. If you do, notice that you have access to the same sorts of tools as in PowerPoint—including the ability to write or draw directly on a slide. This comes in handy if you do, in fact, have a VGA adapter for your PDA. To display your slides via a VGA projector or computer monitor, choose Tools | Options and set up the program using the Output tab. The presentation will look like this on your Pocket PC:

FIND IT ON THE CD

Pocket SlideShow, $19.95
CNetX
www.cnetx.com

4 Minutes of Meeting

Take Control of Your Meeting

Scheduling a meeting is the easy part. In fact, your Pocket PC makes it a snap to add, edit, check, and manage your appointments while you're on the go. But what about when you need to take detailed notes at a meeting, track a series of meetings, or keep minutes that you'll later need to distribute to coworkers? You might turn to a program like Minutes of Meeting, from Dreamee Soft.

This cool little program is designed to let you organize meetings by entering lots of details about the who, what, why, when, and where of your daily activities.

As you can see in the following illustration, Minutes of Meeting allows you to enter details like the time and place of meetings, codes associated with the meeting, and the specific attendees who were at the meeting. It's these kinds of details that are instrumental in making effective notes.

Speaking of notes, Minutes of Meeting has two means of jotting down information about your activities. A NotePad lets you associate free-form notes with each meeting, and a Scribble pad lets you write and draw with digital ink:

FIND IT ON THE CD
Minutes of Meeting, $6.99
Dreamee Soft
www.dreameesoft.com

5 PocketPrint

Print a Document

The ultimate handheld PC would probably look a lot like the Pocket PC that's already in your pocket, but with one important difference: it would have a paper-thin printer embedded inside, enabling you to print anything you see on the screen. While that's mere science fiction for the time being, this doesn't mean you can't print stuff from a PDA. Quite the contrary: armed with a print program, you can send a wide variety of documents from your Pocket PC to a desktop printer or to a portable, pocket-sized printer.

But therein lies the rub—in order to print anything from your PDA, you need to add a print program, since Microsoft didn't build a print driver into the Pocket PC operating system. We use Anycom's PocketPrint, since it can print just about any kind of document to just about any kind of printer around. To print, just start the program and choose the kind of document that you want to print from the icons at the bottom of the screen. You can print Word, Excel, and e-mail files.

PocketPRINT	9:11	
All Folders ▼		Name ▼
ghtgj.txt	1/22/04	48b
Note1.pwi	9/19/03	2k
ohoarii.pwi	9/16/03	1k
pictureperfect65...	9/29/03	9k
smartphones-gs...	1/22/04	21k
SysInfo.txt	12/29/03	784b
zagat.psw	1/22/04	5k

| Doc Options | | |

The easiest way to print from your Pocket PC to a nearby printer is via infrared. Your PDA's IR port can communicate directly with compatible printers.

If you have a Bluetooth adapter for your Pocket PC, or if you have a model with Bluetooth built in, you might instead want to print wirelessly to a Bluetooth-enabled printer. As we wrote this chapter, our Bluetooth options in the printing world were quite limited, but we expect that will slowly start to change over the next few months. Even if you don't have a printer with Bluetooth built in, you can also get a Bluetooth adapter—it plugs into the printer port behind the printer and lets you access the printer from up to 30 feet away wirelessly from any Bluetooth computer or PDA.

Finding Printers for Your Pocket PC

Intrigued by all this talk of portable printing? It turns out that there's a whole lot of printers that are either small enough to take on the road or have infrared ports for chatting with a PDA. Here's a list of models you might want to consider:

Manufacturer	Printer	Style
Desktop printers with infrared		
Hewlett-Packard	LaserJet 6P	Desktop laser printer
	LaserJet 2100	Desktop laser printer
Portable, laptop-oriented printers		
Canon	BJC-55	Lightweight mobile printer
	BJC-85	Lightweight mobile printer
Handheld-sized portable printers		
Brother	MPrint	Handheld thermal printer
Pentax	PocketJet 200	Handheld thermal printer, compatible with IrDA adapter
SiPix Imaging	Pocket Printer A6	Handheld thermal printer

FIND IT ON THE CD
PocketPrint, $39.95
Anycom
www.anycom.com

6 | IA ScreenShot

Ready for Your Screenshot, Mr. DeMille?

Perhaps you've thumbed through this book, some Pocket PC web sites, or a magazine or two and wondered, "How do all those clever people get images of their Pocket PCs?"

First, thanks for calling us clever. Really, it's only Dave that's clever—Rick is more what we like to call "awaiting his equivalency diploma."

The answer, though, is deceptively simple: we use a screenshot utility that captures Pocket PC displays and lets us copy the files to the PC, where they're ordinary digital images in common file formats like BMP or JPG.

We like IA ScreenShot from IA Style, and you can try it for 15 days using the demo that's on the CD-ROM. When you start the program, you'll want to get it ready for making screenshots by entering the Capture Settings dialog box. Choose Tools | Capture Settings from the menu and you'll see this:

Be sure to enable screen capture by checking the box at the top of the screen. Also, specify what action you want to trigger the screenshot. We set it to button 4, which we don't use often anyway. Configure anything else you like on this page (such as the default folder for storing your screenshots on the Pocket PC).

What file format do you want to store your screenshots in? JPG is a good choice since it is compressed and makes small files. To set the file format, tap the Change button next to Filename and then select the capture file format. Tap OK to close this dialog box.

When you're ready to close the Capture Settings dialog box, tap OK.

Now capture a screen. Set up the Pocket PC to suit your needs and click the screen capture button. When you put the PDA in its ActiveSync cradle, open the folder in which you're storing the images and drag them onto the Windows desktop. You're done!

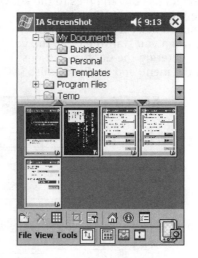

Killer Tip   *Some Pocket PC screens are less than cooperative. Suppose you want to capture an open menu, for instance—tapping the screenshot button may unintentionally close the menu before it's captured. Easy solution: use IA ScreenShot's delay option. With a 10- or 20-second delay, for instance, you can start the capture, set up your screen, and wait for it to be grabbed.*

FIND IT ON THE CD
IA ScreenShot, $9.95
IA Style
www.iastyle.com

7 PIToday

One Glance to See It All

The Pocket PC Today screen is a great idea—it's one place you can go to find out what's going on in your day. And since it's usually the first thing you see when you turn on your PDA, it's a real boon for folks that need a little organization in their lives.

Our only complaint? It doesn't show enough information. And it's not configurable enough. Okay, that's two complaints—but we satisfied them both with one program. Try PI*Today* and we think you'll be amazed at the difference. PI*Today* truly lets you take charge of your tasks, appointments, and e-mails with a better Today screen. Here's a typical view of PI*Today:*

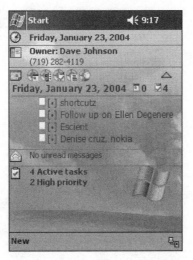

And that's not all—PI*Today* makes the Today screen truly interactive. Tap and hold to get context-sensitive menus with gobs of options for customizing the display and changing the options:

The real power of PI*Today* comes from its many options. To get started, choose Settings from the Pocket PC's Start menu and tap on the Today icon. Tap the Items tab, and select PI*Today*. Finally, tap the Options button, and you'll be dropped into PI*Today's* many-tabbed options. You can control a huge number of features, including whether appointments and tasks are displayed, the layout and look of appointments, how tasks are sorted, and how information on the Today screen is filtered.

Killer Tip *Want to find more information on your PDA about something on your PI Today screen? Tap and hold the item and select Search Subject from the menu.*

FIND IT ON THE CD
PI*Today*, $10
DeJe Online
www.pitoday.de.vu

8 Pocket Outliner

Outline Your Thoughts and Ideas

Everyone has a little genius hidden away in them. At least, that's what Rick's mom told him when he accidentally put his pants on backwards. Last week. Nonetheless, getting your spark of brilliance out of your head and onto paper, into PowerPoint, or in whatever vehicle will get you promoted to company VP sometimes takes a little coaxing. The Pocket PC's NotePad or even Pocket Word may be fine for writing down your ideas in a linear way, but it's weak when it comes to rearranging and fine tuning those ideas. Instead, try an idea organizer.

Pocket Outliner, from DSRTech, is an ideal way to articulate and polish ideas, projects, outlines, and other day-to-day documents. Pocket Outliner is, as the name suggests, an outliner—it lets you "nest" your ideas into a structure that represents the way the data in your head is actually related and connected. Imagine you're outlining a tip report. You might make these notes in your PDA:

Exec Meeting

- ■ Vision statement
- ■ Approved upgrades

Factory Tour

- ■ Can we get a pool table like theirs?
- ■ Innovative security
    - ■ Eye scanners
    - ■ Passive card readers

Once you are back on your desktop, you can obviously hone these notes into a complete report. But it's obviously easier with an organized outline that you've been able to complete on your PDA. Here's how to do it with Pocket Outliner:

1. Start the program and tap New. This begins a new project.

2. Enter a name for this outline in the space that currently says Change Outline Name.

3. To make your first entry, tap the colored boxes at the bottom of the screen. Then enter information on this new line.

4. The next time you create a new entry, it will be nested under the first one you just created. To "promote" this item to a main heading, tap the left-pointing arrow at the bottom of the screen.

5. From here out, you can add new entries and use the four arrow buttons at the bottom of the screen to indent, nest, move, and rearrange items to your heart's content. When you want to copy the project to the PC, tap Tools | Export and save the file as either a text or HTML file on the Pocket PC. You can later drag and drop that file onto your Windows desktop, where you can use it in any program you like.

FIND IT ON THE CD
Pocket Outliner, $12.99
DSRTech
www.dsrtech.net

9 powerOne Finance

Perform Complex Calculations

Looking for a better calculator? No, it's not quite as exciting as a better music player, a better car, or a better mousetrap. But the calculator that comes with your PDA is pretty anemic—it adds, subtracts, multiplies, and divides. (If you didn't know there was a calculator in your PDA, just look for a program called Calculator in the Programs folder—it's not much, but it's there.)

If you want to do more, you need to add a new calculator to your device.

powerOne Finance, from Infinity Softworks, is no doubt the best calculator package available for the Pocket PC. You owe it to yourself to try the demo on this CD. It includes all of the financial functions of traditional business calculators, like the HP 12C, HP 17B, HP19B, and TI-BAII+. It's also highly customizable. Long-time HP users will no doubt appreciate the RPN (Reverse Polish Notation) input. If you're more familiar with scientific calculators, you will prefer Order of Operation input (as in 3+4*5 = 23). Last, but not least, financial calculator users will default to the Chain input method (3+4*5 = 35).

There's also a wide array of prebuilt equations in a number of categories. There are Calendar calculations (such as finding the difference between two dates), unit conversions, business math (like finding discounts, markups, profit margins, tax, and tip), and custom calculation templates.

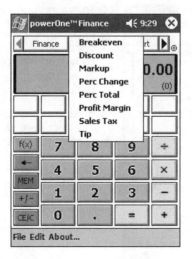

These equations are very powerful and worth the price of the calculator alone, especially if you find yourself frequently needing to find metric equivalents or the percent change between numbers.

FIND IT ON THE CD
powerOne Finance, $59.99
Infinity Softworks
www.infinitysw.com

10 MobileDB

Databases to Go

Your PDA is a great place to keep track of data—personal information, customer or client data, field research, you name it. If you've ever thought that your Pocket PC was a smart place to track information but you didn't want to use a free-form text file like the Memo Pad, then a database application might be right for you.

Handmark's MobileDB is a great database application to get your feet wet in mobile databases. Using MobileDB, you can create your own databases, reference databases that have been made elsewhere in your company, download new ones from the Web, and more. How to get started? Easy. After you install MobileDB, just follow these steps to create your own database:

1. When you start MobileDB, you see a list of all the database files stored on your PDA. You can tap any one of them to open and review the data.

2. To create a new database from scratch, tap New.

3. In the Create Database dialog box, enter a name. Suppose we're going to make a database to collect information about customer satisfaction as we travel from client to client. Name this database Client Satisfaction and click OK.

4. We'd like there to be three fields in this database. The first field will be the client's name. The second field will store the kind of equipment that is installed. The third field will be a record of the customer satisfaction on a scale of one to ten. On the Field Definitions screen, enter **Client** in the space for Field 1.

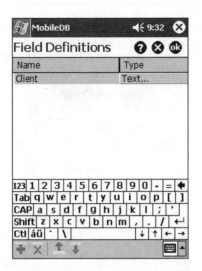

5. Tap the Plus symbol at the bottom of the screen to create a new field.

6. In Field 2, enter **Equipment**.

7. Again, tap the Plus symbol.

8. Finally, for Field 3, enter **Satisfaction** and change the type of field from Text to Number. Tap OK.

9. You are now taken to the database itself. You can enter data by tapping the New button and tapping Done when the data is complete. Here you can see a completed database with information stored within:

FIND IT ON THE CD
MobileDB, $29.99
Handmark
www.handmark.com

11 RepliGo

Put a PDF in Your Pocket

Even though your Pocket PC has applications like Pocket Word and Pocket Excel for carting around common business applications, things aren't peachy enough to make a pie. After all, you already know that your Pocket PC strips away a lot of formatting information when you use Pocket Word, and there are certain kinds of documents that just don't fit in your PDA anyway. Consider the good old PDF file, for instance. Also called Adobe Acrobat files, these documents are the mainstay of any office. PDFs get traded around like some sort of high-tech, buisnessy baseball cards, and everyone is expected to be able to read them. That's great if you're in the office, but what if you are on the go? Can you copy a PDF file to your PDA and read it on the train, in a plane, or sunbathing on the yacht?

Sure you can. Get RepliGo from Cerience. RepliGo is a powerful document converter that lets you convert virtually any document—Word, Excel, PDF, web pages, PowerPoint, even Microsoft Project files—into a form that can be viewed on the PDA. In the process, nothing is lost. Indeed, on the Pocket PC, documents look virtually identical to their desktop cousins. You can zoom in for a better view or zoom out and take in all (or most) of the document at once.

Here's how to create and view a PDF file on your Pocket PC after installing RepliGo:

1. Open a PDF file on your desktop computer.

2. Choose File | Print to see the Print dialog box.

3. From the list of available printers, choose RepliGo.

4. Specify the print range. If you want to convert the entire document to a RepliGo file and view it on the PDA, click OK. Otherwise, select just the page or pages you want to transfer.

5. After the "printing" process, you'll see a Convert Document dialog box. You can change the document's name (as it appears on the Pocket PC), specify the location—handheld or memory card—and then click OK.

6. After the conversion, perform an ActiveSync.

7. Open RepliGo and choose the file from the list. Now you can use the controls at the bottom of the screen to read and navigate the document.

FIND IT ON THE CD
RepliGo, $29.95
Cerience
www.cerience.com

12 PocketPrivacy

For Your Eyes Only

The data on your PDA is inherently insecure. If you ever lose your Pocket PC, then all of your contact data, personal information, and everything else on the device will be available to anyone who finds it. The price of your PDA itself is small in comparison to the loss of your data if it falls into the wrong hands.

That's why we recommend that you try a program like PocketPrivacy, from PocketMind. PocketPrivacy is designed to hide the data on your PDA; if you don't know the password, you can't see your data. Note that PocketPrivacy doesn't really encrypt anything; it just makes it look like there's nothing there to find to begin with.

After you install the program, you can find it lurking in Settings. Choose Settings from the menu and then tap on the System tab. Start PocketPrivacy.

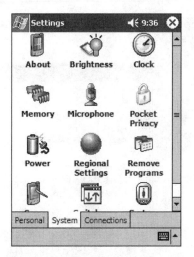

The first thing you should do is enter and verify a password. Without a password, anyone can pick up your Pocket PC and disable PocketPrivacy, revealing all your hidden data—and that would defeat the purpose of the program.

The program is divided into a number of tabs. The first tab is where you can globally hide or show all of your data. If you've already hidden appointments, for instance, and now want to see them, tap Show All in the Outlook Data section, then close the program.

On the successive tabs, you can selectively show or hide any contacts, appointments, tasks, notes, programs, and even specific files. Just be sure that when you decide to make a change, you tap the Apply button on that tabbed screen—otherwise, your change will not take effect.

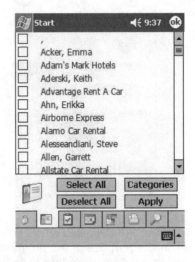

FIND IT ON THE CD
PocketPrivacy, $24.95
PocketMind
www.pocketmind.com

13 myCard

Abracadabra—Was That Your Card?

Have you noticed how easily Palm OS folks share contact information? They tap one button to beam their "business card" to another Palm, and can send and receive Outlook contacts without any trouble at all. If only it were that easy for your Pocket PC. Well, now it is. Try myCard (developed by Pedro Ivo Faria), a ridiculously cheap program (it's just $4.95) that helps automate sending and receiving Outlook contact data.

Here's how it works: when you first install the program, you need to create a business card (really, just a contact for the Contacts program) or designate an existing contact as your business card.

After that, you'll see a simple screen that is designed to facilitate either sending or receiving business cards.

If you want to beam your card to any PDA, tap Send My Card and the contact info you previously set up will be beamed to the other device. If you want to get someone's contact information, tap the section called Receive a Card and point your Pocket PC in their general direction. That's all there is to it!

Killer Tip *The other PDA does not have to have MyCard installed in order to receive a card sent from your Pocket PC with MyCard.*

FIND IT ON THE CD
myCard, $4.95
Pedro Ivo Faria
www.handango.com

Chapter 2

Bon Voyage!

As far as Rick is concerned, the only thing better than traveling is traveling light. Pocket PC PDAs are ideal in that regard, as they enable you to carry books for reading, music for listening, movies for watching—and all the important items you need when taking a trip. We're talking reservation information, language dictionaries, street maps, even guides to local restaurants and hot spots. Why stuff all that stuff in your carry-on bag when you can pack it in your PDA instead?

14 Vindigo

Concierge in Your Pocket

POWER APP Vindigo is the ultimate travel accessory. It provides up-to-the-minute dining, shopping, entertainment, and other leisure information for over 50 major U.S. cities (see the Vindigo web site for a complete list) and London. With just a tap or two, you can find restaurants and reviews, ATMs, bookstores, bars, clubs, flower shops, maps, movie theaters and show times, and plenty more. It even provides local weather and step-by-step walking directions from your current location to any other location in its database.

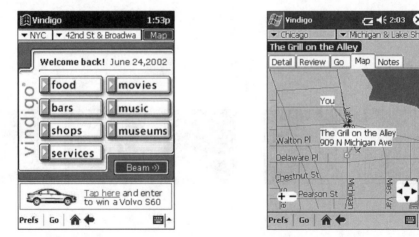

The service isn't free, but it's definitely affordable. You can pay a $3.50 monthly fee or subscribe for an entire year for $24.95.

Killer Tip *As with many Pocket PC programs, you can try Vindigo before plunking down your hard-earned moola. The service offers a free 30-day trial version, which should give you ample opportunity to evaluate it. We think if you travel a lot or live in a big city, Vindigo is well worth the price of admission.*

So how does all this information get from Vindigo to your PDA? After you perform the initial installation of the software and set up your account, you use a Web-based interface (see Figure 2-1) to choose which city (or cities) you want to include. Within each city, you can add or remove content channels—subsets of information, such as food, shops, movies, and services. (Each channel consumes some of your PDA's memory, so if there's information you don't necessarily need, it's best to deselect it.)

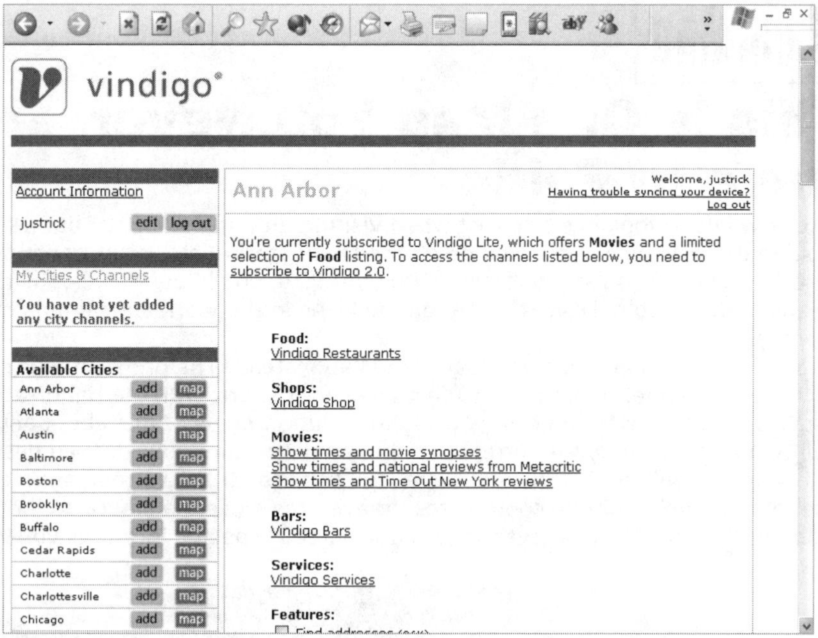

FIGURE 2-1   You manage your Vindigo account at the company's web site, where you choose desired cities and content channels for each one.

With all those steps done and choices made, all that remains is to ActiveSync. Each time you do, your PC will connect to Vindigo's servers, download up-to-date information, and then copy it to your PDA. This is a pretty cool approach, as it eliminates the need for you to have a wireless or Internet-connected PDA. Instead, it takes advantage of your computer's existing Internet connection.

Killer Tip   *If you do have a wireless or Internet-connected PDA, you can use it to download updated listings wherever you are—no PC required.*

Much of Vindigo's power lies in its street-level maps, which enable you to navigate to any destination from your current location. In fact, if you tap the Go tab, Vindigo will generate step-by-step walking directions (you can use them for driving as well, but the assumption is that if you're in a big city, you're probably on foot).

Killer Tip   *When viewing Vindigo listings, look for text that's underscored with a solid blue line. These are links (much like the kind you find in your web browser): when you tap one, you're taken to related information for that item, or given a map-related option if it's a street.*

FIND IT

Vindigo, $24.95 annual subscription
Vindigo
www.vindigo.com

15 HandMap

This Is One Map You Never Have to Fold

No one wants to look like a tourist when visiting an unfamiliar city, but it's hard to avoid that image when you walk down the street staring at a giant paper map. On the other hand, if you're interacting with your PDA, you'll look hip, sophisticated, and urbane (unless you're Dave, that is—all the PDAs in the world ain't gonna make that happen).

So skip the paper maps and load HandMap instead. The program bills itself as an "electronic street directory," but that's selling it short. With the HandMap viewer installed on your PDA, you can view high-resolution maps of just about any city or county. You can mark your current position on a map and your desired destination, and HandMap will help guide you there. You can search for a street, an intersection, a set of latitude/longitude coordinates, or even the closest restaurants, hotels, and shopping centers. You can even record notes about specific locations you've visited.

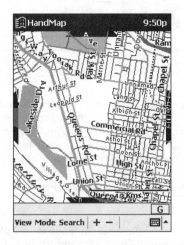

To get started with HandMap, you must first purchase the viewer, which sells for $16. Next, you'll need maps, which are available from the HandMap web site, with prices ranging from around $8 for a set of five county maps (over 3,000 U.S. counties are available) to $28 for a set of 30 U.S. cities. (The site is also home to maps of Canadian cities, Singapore, and South America.) If you're lucky enough to have a GPS receiver that works with your PDA, you can also purchase a software plug-in ($10) that adds GPS capabilities to HandMap. Instead of having to manually pinpoint your location on a map, the receiver will do it for you.

Killer Tip   *For more information on using GPS with your PDA, Rick shamefully recommends* How to Do Everything with Your GPS *(2004, McGraw-Hill/Osborne), which he wrote.*

At this point, you're probably wondering just how useful a map can be when it's no larger than three inches—the size of your PDA's screen. Think about this: when you look at a paper map, don't you usually focus on one small area? At that point, the rest of the map becomes fairly superfluous. In any case, with HandMap you can scroll around to find the area of the map you need, then zoom in or out depending on the desired level of detail.

Killer Tip *If you're not used to electronic maps, zooming can be a hard concept to grasp. Use HandMap's onscreen zoom tool (the plus and minus buttons) to experiment with magnification.*

Scrolling is best accomplished in the software's Drag mode, which can be selected by tapping Mode | Drag. Once you've loaded a map, zoom down to around a 0.3- or 0.1-mile level. Now tap the center of the screen with your stylus, hold it down, and drag the stylus around. You'll see the map scroll in whatever direction you drag the stylus. In Normal mode, dragging your stylus around reveals the names of streets and places. Scrolling is accomplished via your PDA's d-pad controller or the scroll bars at the edges of the screen (tap one to scroll in that direction).

Want to search for a street name, intersection, or some other map feature? Just tap HandMap's Search option, choose the type of search you want, then fill in the corresponding data.

This is one of those programs that's not exactly ideal for novices, but with a little practice and experimentation, you should be able to put it to good use. Make sure to print a copy of the instruction manual, which is available on the HandMap web site: www.handmap.net/WinCE/map-guide.htm.

FIND IT ON THE CD
HandMap, $16 plus maps
HandMap
www.handmap.net

16 Zagat To Go

Zagat's the Way We Like It (Uh-Huh, Uh-Huh)

While Dave's idea of fine dining is an all-you-can-eat salad bar, Rick prefers restaurants with cloth napkins, a wine list, maybe even valet parking. You probably know the best places to eat in your neck of the woods, but what about when you're traveling in an unfamiliar city—or you live in a place like New York or Chicago, where the restaurants outnumber the people? In those cases, a dining guide can come in awfully handy.

In case you're not familiar with Zagat, it began as a New York–centric dining guidebook with restaurant ratings provided by actual customers, not critics with their fancy palettes. Eventually the guide evolved and expanded, culminating with Zagat To

Go 2004: a Pocket PC version that includes guides for about 35 cities, each one containing food, décor, and service ratings for various upscale restaurants.

After you download the trial version (or subscribe to the service, which is continually updated and costs $24.95 per year), you'll then visit the Zagat To Go web site to choose which cities and guides to install on your PDA. (In addition to restaurant reviews, the service now includes Lifestyle and Nightlife guides—but only for a few cities.)

Using Zagat To Go is quite simple: just select the city or guide you want to view, then choose your sorting option from the pop-up menu. You can sort by favorites, most popular, type of cuisine, and so on. When you see a restaurant that's of interest, tap it to view its details, ratings, and review. Zagat ratings are on a scale of 0–30. Here's a quick reference key you can use to understand the listings:

- **F** Food
- **D** Décor
- **S** Service
- **C** Cost (the estimated price of dinner for one with one drink and the tip)

Killer Tip *Be sure you download and install the 14-day trial version before subscribing to Zagat To Go to make sure the service offers enough restaurants in your city—or the cities you plan to visit—to make the purchase worthwhile. For instance, it lists only about 20 restaurants for all of Detroit and the surrounding suburbs, which is where Rick lives. And Zagat serves just five locations for Dave's hometown of Colorado Springs.*

FIND IT ON THE CD

Zagat To Go 2004, $24.95 (CD or download, one-year subscription)
Zagat
www.zagat.com

17 Voice Translator Multilingual Edition

Parlez-Vous Pocket PC? Let Your PDA Do the Talking

We don't know about you, but we've forgotten most of the French we learned in high school (sorry, Mrs. Herman!). So it was a little embarrassing when we visited Paris and asked to buy a "purple monkey dishwasher" from a fruit stand. We could have avoided this "faux pas" (that's French for "elevator chimney") with a program like the Speereo Voice Translator Multilingual Edition, which includes over 4,000 common phrases and can actually speak them aloud! That certainly beats fumbling your way through a French dictionary and then butchering the words you're trying to pronounce. See Figure 2-2 for an example of the program's easy-to-use interface.

FIGURE 2-2   With the Speereo Voice Translator, you simply tap the word or phrase you want spoken, or say it aloud in English!

Voice Translator speaks not only French, but also German, Spanish, Italian, and Russian. More remarkable still, the software recognizes spoken English, meaning you can talk into your Pocket PC, and Voice Translator will repeat the phrase in the desired language. Here's an example of how it works:

1. In the categorized lists of phrases, find the one you want translated.

2. Press and hold your Pocket PC's microphone record button.

3. Say the phrase in your normal speaking voice. Voice Translator will repeat the phrase in whatever language you've selected. Is that cool or what!

Killer Tip   *You can also tap any phrase with the stylus and get the same result. In case the person you're trying to communicate with doesn't understand Voice Translator's voice (it's surprisingly good, but still a little, uh, computery), you can show him or her the screen—the translated phrase appears as text at the top.*

If you like the idea of a talking phrasebook but don't need so many languages, check out MobiLearn's Outloud! Talking Phrasebook (www.mobilearn.net). MobiLearn uses real human voices—recorded in high-quality MP3—to help get you through any international incident.

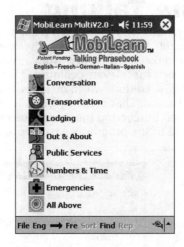

In addition to Outloud's 400 standard expressions, MobiLearn sells phrasebooks in categories like travel, dating, driving, and cuisine, all for about $16 each. (We think the English-to-French dating phrasebook is just wishful thinking, but the option is there if you're an optimist.) Phrasebooks are also available in German, Italian, and Spanish.

The audio is crystal clear, and the database is easily searchable—two big plusses. But there's no way for foreigners to respond in English, which is a shame. Of course, the same is true of Voice Translator, so we recommend you try both to see which you like best.

18 | Pocket Travel Dictionary

Foreign Languages Made Easy

Talking phrasebooks are all well and good when you're visiting a foreign country, but sometimes you just need a dictionary. That's where the aptly named Pocket Travel Dictionary comes in. Far easier to search than a paper-based dictionary (and requiring a lot less space in your carry-on bag), Pocket Travel Dictionary is available in ten different language pairs. Most of them are English and another language, such as French, German, Italian, Spanish, or Dutch. But the company also offers French-German, French-Spanish, and Spanish-German dictionaries. ¡Ay caramba!

To look up any word, simply write it in the Search For field (using the data-entry method of your choice), then tap Find. After Pocket Travel Dictionary locates the translations, you can use the Copy Selection to Clipboard function on any of the found words, then paste that word into a memo, e-mail, or any other program.

19 TripTracker

Don't Let Your Travel Unravel

Travel is an information-intensive task these days, what with all those flight times and hotel reservations and confirmation numbers. TripTracker stores all the details of your air travel, car rentals, and hotel accommodations, thereby turning you into a more organized and better-prepared traveler.

Though you could just as easily jot the same information into a memo, there's something to be said for TripTracker's comprehensive organizational skills. It sorts trips individually; each one can contain as much flight, car, and hotel information as is necessary for the trip (helpful if your journey includes several stops). TripTracker also stores frequent-flyer ID numbers and comes with a currency calculator for travel abroad. There's even a world-clock screen that shows the day and time for up to four different locations.

The software incorporates listings for a multitude of airlines, airports, hotels, and car-rental agencies, but a few of the databases are incomplete. The West Palm Beach airport, for instance, isn't listed. Fortunately, you can add new listings to any category or edit existing listings (just tap and hold with the stylus, then tap Edit).

As an added bonus, TripTracker includes an expense manager. Just tap New | Expense, then enter the details—amount, category, payment method, and so on. As an even bigger bonus, TripTracker comes with a desktop counterpart that not only makes for faster, easier entry of your trip details, but also integrates with Microsoft Outlook. That means when you sync your PDA with your PC, all the trip details you've entered into TripTracker will appear in your calendar.

TripTracker	◀€ 1:32 ✕	
Acme Sales Meeting		Expenses ▾

Date	Description	Amount
~~03/08/2003~~	~~Car Rental~~	~~78.00~~
~~03/18/2003~~	~~Limo~~	~~85.00~~
03/18/2003	Business Meals	55.00
03/18/2003	Lunch	0.00
03/19/2003	Hotel Charges	119.00
03/19/2003	Incidentals	18.75
03/20/2003	Lodging	335.00

New Tools ☽ | 🖼 $€ 🕾 | ⊕ | ⌨ ▲

Needless to say, don't leave home without TripTracker.

FIND IT ON THE CD

TripTracker, $29.95
Two Peaks Solutions
www.twopeaks.com

20 Mapopolis Navigator

Door-to-Door Driving Directions Done Adroitly

This is one of the few times in this book we're going to talk about software that requires additional hardware. The software: Mapopolis Navigator, a street-level mapping program that gives you door-to-door driving directions from point A to point B.

The hardware: a GPS receiver, a device that receives data from Global Positioning System satellites and uses it to determine your position. Put the two together and you can see your location on a moving map, right on your PDA screen.

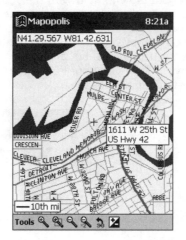

This is pretty cool stuff, but you need to understand a few things before proceeding. For starters, there's the GPS receiver. You can buy one directly from Mapopolis or investigate the products from companies like ALK, Belkin, Delorme, Socket, and TomTom. Many of these come bundled with software other than Mapopolis Navigator, and you may decide to use that software instead. We don't mind—our primary purpose in this section is simply to reveal that your PDA can serve as a very capable navigation tool. The hardware and software are up to you. (For the record, we're particularly fond of the Socket and TomTom bundles.)

That said, if your PDA has a built-in Bluetooth radio (models that do include the iPAQ h1945 and iPAQ h2215), we highly recommend getting a Bluetooth receiver. That way, there's no physical connection required between your PDA and the GPS—and who wants a cable flopping around your car's dashboard?

Killer Tip *Check eBay and other online sources for Bluetooth GPS receivers. Even if you buy one that's designed for Palm handhelds, it should still work with your Pocket PC model. That's part of the beauty of Bluetooth: it's platform-agnostic. You may be able to save big bucks by picking up a used receiver or last year's model.*

Now let's talk about Mapopolis Navigator. It's a fairly capable program, offering features like on-the-fly driving directions (meaning you choose your destination right on your PDA—no computer required—and Navigator immediately generates the directions) and voice-prompted driving directions (your PDA actually speaks to you, telling you which way to go, when to turn, and so on). But the software can be a bit confusing to use, starting with the maps themselves.

Navigator itself is free; you can download it from the Mapopolis web site or find it on this book's CD. However, it's of no use without maps. Mapopolis sells a Navigator Map Pack, which contains street maps for all of North America, for $99.95. You can also purchase individual county maps for around $10 each. We find this a really annoying approach, as it requires you to know the name of each and every county you're going to pass through on the way to your destination. Needless to say, you're probably better off buying the Map Pack—but even then you have to know which counties to load on your PDA. Blech.

You'll also want to make sure you have enough storage space on your PDA for the map files, which can be quite large. The map for Oakland County, Michigan, where Rick lives, nabs more than three megabytes' worth of memory. Fortunately, you can load maps onto a memory card, which we strongly recommend.

Killer Tip *For more information on using GPS with your PDA, Rick shamefully recommends* How to Do Everything with Your GPS *(2004, McGraw-Hill/Osborne), which he wrote. It's even more shameful now because it's the second time he's recommended it in this chapter.*

Killer Tip *If you don't want to incur the expense of a GPS receiver or deal with the complexity of Mapopolis, you can still get door-to-door driving directions on your PDA. All you need is AvantGo (see Chapter 9), which can download directions created at the MapQuest web site.*

FIND IT ON THE CD
Mapopolis Navigator, Free (maps extra)
Mapopolis
www.mapopolis.com

Make a Backup

Surprisingly few PDA users bother to back up their devices, relying solely on desktop synchronization for retaining programs and data. But what happens when you're on the road and disaster strikes? You could find yourself bereft of important documents, phone numbers, appointment data—the works.

There are several backup utilities available for Pocket PC handhelds, but we've yet to find a more simplistic and all-encompassing solution than Mobile Digital Media's Secure File PDA Backup (www.gomdm.com). This 64MB memory card comes with a program called Sprite Backup. Just pop it into your PDA's SD slot and the utility loads automatically. From there it's a simple matter to back up your entire PDA—or restore it again should the need arise.

If you follow just one tip in this entire book, make it this one. Make regular backups!

Chapter 3

Gone Fishin'

Y ou know the future has arrived when a device the size of a deck of cards can hold a handful of Stephen King novels, the full contents of a photo album, a few of your favorite songs, and perhaps even a Hollywood movie or a television show. Don't look so surprised: your Pocket PC is great for all sorts of multimedia tricks.

And your PDA finally makes this sort of thing practical. Before the Pocket PC came along, for instance, a slowly growing collection of electronic books—mostly public-domain classic literature, like Voltaire's *Candide* and Sir Arthur Conan Doyle's *Sherlock Holmes* stories—existed on the Internet. But your PDA makes them convenient to read anytime, anywhere. Your PDA also makes it easy to watch movies and listen to music on an airplane or train. And just one device does it all. In this chapter, we'll check out the most exciting apps you need to make this work.

21 | Veo Photo Traveler

Take a Picture

There was a time when only James Bond had access to all the coolest spy gear, but the times they are a-changin'. These days, many PDAs and cell phones have digital cameras built right in, for instance, making it easy to snap photos anytime, anywhere. The camera as we know it just might be extinct.

But what if your existing Pocket PC doesn't have a digital camera built in? That's easy—you can add one. Veo Photo Traveler for Pocket PC is a camera-on-a-CompactFlash card designed for certain Pocket PC models like iPAQ, Toshiba, and Casio models. The camera itself has a rotating head that lets you shoot toward or away from the PDA's LCD screen and it captures still images at resolutions from 160×120 to 640×480 pixels. There's also a video mode: you can grab AVI movies with or without sound in either 160×120 or 320×240 pixels. Camera controls include a self-timer and white balance adjustment—all the basics you need to take snapshots with your Pocket PC. You can see the little gem right here:

The camera also comes with all the software you need to spy on foreign dignitaries and e-mail the results from your PC. An album viewer makes it easy to review your pictures and videos on your Pocket PC, and there's also a desktop application with a suite of tools for copying images and videos between the PDA and Windows, and for making movies, e-cards, and simple web pages. The movie maker lets you combine multiple video clips, trim them, add titles and transitions, and even attach WAV soundtracks. Not bad for an $80 camera kit.

FIND IT ON THE CD
Veo Photo Traveler, $79.99 ($99 version for the Dell Axim available, as well)
Veo
www.veo.com

22 Flip It!

Make an Animation

It has been said that Walt Disney got his start by drawing animations of Mickey Mouse on his PDA. It has only been said by us, though, since the PDA hadn't even been invented when old Walt was doodling his first cartoons. But that shouldn't stop you from making your own animations on your PDA.

But how, you ask? With Flip It!, a great little $5 animation program—the demo, which limits you to ten frames of animation, is included on the CD.

Flip It! makes it amazingly easy to create animations using a technique known as onion skinning—when you draw a frame of animation, you can see a light impression of the previous frame's drawing at the same time. That makes it a snap to draw images that move, jiggle, gyrate, dance, and prance across the PDA's screen.

As you can see from the simple Flip It! screen, you can control the brush size and ink color from the two tabs on the sides of the screen, and step through the animation via the controls at the bottom. The major application controls—like loading and saving animations—are accessed from the tab at the top.

Making an animation is a snap. Just start drawing—you start on the first frame of your animation. When you're done, tap the next cell button (the second button from the right) and you'll see the second frame with a light impression of the drawing on frame one.

Make your drawing on the next frame and then step through the frames, adding to your drawing and animation as you see fit. You can go backwards and change frames any time you like.

When you're ready, tap the Play button to see your complete animation. It's fun and addictive!

FIND IT ON THE CD

Flip It!, $4.99
Digital Concepts
www.dig-concepts.com

23 Pocket Artist

Paint a Pretty Picture

You're probably wondering why you might want to paint on a handheld computer so small that it fits in your pocket. Well, in the world of computers, the answer is often "because you can." Programmers have never let something as silly as a technical limitation get in the way of doing something, so when PDAs first came out, programmers seemed to scramble to become the first to create a paint program for their favorite handheld PC.

But, aside from that admittedly flippant answer, the capability to sketch things out on your Pocket PC is a handy feature. You can draw a map to sketch the way to lunch, outline a process, or design a flowchart. You can also just doodle—use the PDA as a high-tech Etch a Sketch for those boring times when you're waiting for the train or pretending to take notes in a meeting. Perhaps most importantly, you can draw on top of pictures you've stored on your PDA, giving you the ability to annotate images and add captions.

Believe it or not, many painting and drawing applications are available for the Pocket PC. Indeed, if you're an adventurous sort of person, search the archives of a software web site like www.pocketgear.com for painting programs, and you'll be amazed by what you find. Nonetheless, our hands-down favorite is a program called, simply enough, Pocket Artist, from Conduits Technologies, shown here:

Certainly the most full-featured PDA paint program we've ever seen, Pocket Artist pretty much does it all. The program has a complete set of painting tools, including a variety of brushes (paintbrush, pencil, and airbrush). The program includes a clone tool, gradient fill feature, and selection tools that include the ability to feather your edges. It's not quite like having Photoshop on your Pocket PC, but it isn't too far off.

Painting on your PDA is fun and can possibly be productive, but you need to remember a couple of limitations. Most importantly, you're working with a resolution of just 320×240 pixels. That just doesn't give you a lot of room in which to draw. After your images are transferred to a PC, you'll find that they're still quite small. So, drawing something on the PDA that you plan to export later to, say, a PowerPoint presentation, generally isn't a practical plan. And even more importantly, few paint programs support printing directly from the Pocket PC.

FIND IT ON THE CD
Pocket Artist, $49.95
Conduits Technologies
www.conduits.com

24 resco Picture Viewer

A Photo Album in Your Pocket

Have you ever noticed how seemingly essential technology often starts as a novelty, but quickly becomes commonplace? Ten years ago, for instance, laser pointers and cell phones attracted so much attention that they were a distraction; today, the business world is full of both of them and no one gives either a second thought. PDA image viewers used to turn heads as well—and not necessarily in a good way. Two years ago,

POWER APP

people thought it was goofy and geeky to look at pictures on a PDA. These days, folks use programs like resco Picture Viewer to show off the grandkids on their Pocket PC. We've included it on the CD so you can try it yourself.

resco Picture Viewer puts everything into an attractive shell. A gorgeous, button-laden startup screen lets you choose from among common tasks like Open Album or Browse CompactFlash Card. resco makes it easy to create many independent photo albums, either from scratch or based on existing folders of images. And Picture Viewer can generate an album directly from a CompactFlash card—just pull a memory card out of your digital camera, insert it into your PDA, and you'll be able to view your images instantly.

Creating a slideshow is easy. Try this: pop a CompactFlash card into your PDA and tap Browse CF Card on the main screen. Then tap Photo | Start Slide Show from the menu.

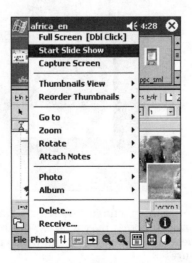

In the Start Slide Show dialog box, you can choose from a library of about a dozen transitions. Effects like fade and dissolve are the most effective, but you can also set the slideshow to randomize the between-slide effects.

Once an album is open, four image thumbnails appear filmstrip-style across the top of the screen, with a larger view of one image in the main part of the display. resco Picture Viewer has a wealth of tools, including a screen capture tool and an elaborate suite of structured and freehand drawing tools to edit your images. You can annotate images with voice notes that play back during the slideshow and you can choose an MP3 or WAV file to become the soundtrack whenever you play that slideshow.

You can also flip and rotate pictures, zoom, and even draw on files to add personal annotations. The program supports over a dozen common file formats—including BMP, GIF, JPG, and MPEG video, which means you can watch movies from within the program as well as browse pictures.

FIND IT ON THE CD
resco Picture Viewer, $19.95
resco
www.resco-net.com

25 Z4Music

Bang the Drums All Day Long

Todd Rundgren can finally have his wish come true (you know, that one about not wanting to work and just wanting to bang the drums all day). If he gets himself a Pocket PC and Z4Music, he can sit around at the bus stop, in train stations, on the back deck, or in his living room and compose drum patterns on his PDA. Z4Music is a simple but highly effective music sequencer for the Pocket PC. It was designed especially for creating drum loops and playing them back on the Pocket PC's speakers or through an amplifier for use as a drum machine as part of a live performance. Yeah, you read that right—your Pocket PC can be an instrument in a band.

The program looks like any drum machine or sequencer—just on a small, handheld screen:

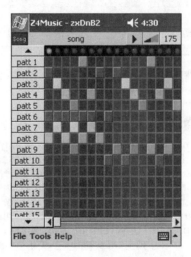

There are two levels of control in Z4Music—the pattern screen and the song screen. When you start the program, you start at the song level, seeing blocks that represent the overall rhythm of the song. Each block is actually a combination of patterns, though—it might include a kick drum, snares, and hi-hats, all arranged to play in a particular pattern over the course of four beats of music. So when you see the song screen, you're seeing the overall "map" to the song.

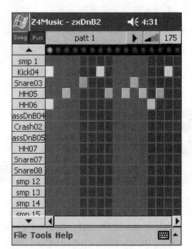

To see the pattern screen, tap one of the pattern headings on the left side of the screen. The display then changes to let you see which instruments play in what arrangement and rhythm. You can create a pattern just by tapping on empty boxes in the pattern screen; to remove a box, tap that space again. To hear what you've created, tap the Play button at the top of the screen.

Killer Tip *Want some drum accompaniment for guitar practice? Just plug your Pocket PC's headphone output into the input of your stereo and play. There's even a basic rock rhythm included with Z4Music—choose File | Open from the menu.*

FIND IT ON THE CD
Z4Music, $9
Z4Soft
www.z4soft.com

26 Pocket Chord Finder

Name That Chord!

Luckily, Boston frontman Tom Shotz—an electrical engineer who is as famous for his inventions as he is for his role in rock and roll—has made it okay to be both a guitarist and a tech geek. Which is why you should always have your Pocket PC nearby if you play guitar. Why? All kinds of reasons, really. Your Pocket PC can help you tune your guitar, for starters. Guitar Tuner, from Implicit Software (www.implicitsoftware.com), allows you to tune your guitar in a variety of ways. This program features nine different tuning settings, with onscreen buttons that correspond to the strings on your guitar. Just tap a button to hear a clear guitar sound and tune your instrument:

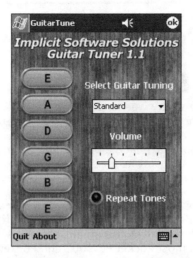

Once you have your guitar tuned, you'll want to try out Pocket Chord Finder. This program is ideal for anyone who is always looking for new, more challenging chords to learn. Just choose a key from the list on the right and customize the chord however you like—minor, major, 6th, 7th—all the common forms are there, and many uncommon forms as well. You can also specify which fret the chord is based on. Finally, you can display a left- or right-handed chord and see the fingering or notes onscreen:

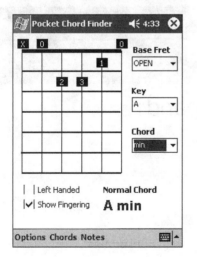 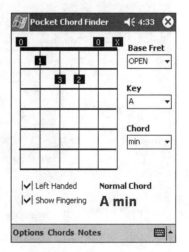

FIND IT ON THE CD
Pocket Chord Finder, $9.99
Rock Stevens Software
www.rockstevens.com

27 Microsoft Reader

Read an E-Book

Here's a recipe for a leisurely weekend: grab your Pocket PC, lie down on the couch, and spend the afternoon reading a novel. Thanks to e-books, you can put a handful of books on your PDA and read them at your leisure.

Thankfully, Microsoft has made e-book reading simple. Almost every Pocket PC available comes with Microsoft Reader, the definitive e-book reader (see Figure 3-1)—and if yours doesn't, just install the one we've provided for you on the CD or check the Microsoft web site for the latest version.

If you already have Microsoft Reader installed, it may still not be the latest version, though. Since Microsoft occasionally updates Microsoft Reader, it's good to know that you can update it with the latest and greatest features. Microsoft Reader for Pocket PC comes preinstalled on most Pocket PC 2002 and Pocket PC 2003 devices. If you already

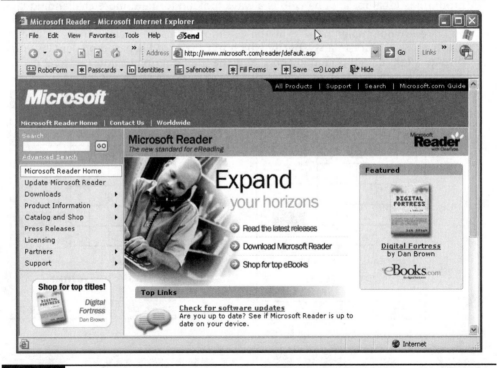

FIGURE 3-1   The Microsoft Reader web site is where you can download the latest version of the app and find out about e-books to download.

have Microsoft Reader installed on your Pocket PC, you'll need to uninstall it before you can put the latest version on your device. Here's what to do:

1. Open the Settings on your Pocket PC by choosing it from the Start menu.

2. Choose the System tab, and then tap Remove Programs.

3. Look for Microsoft Reader. If you can't find Microsoft Reader in the list of applications at all, that's okay. It means the program is installed in ROM, so it can't be deleted. You can just install the latest version of Microsoft Reader by skipping down to step 5.

4. If you see Microsoft Reader in the list, tap it, and then tap the Remove button. After a few moments, it should be gone from your device.

5. Place the Pocket PC in its cradle and turn it on. Be sure that ActiveSync starts and that the PDA is communicating with the PC.

6. Download the latest version of Microsoft Reader from Microsoft's web site.

7. When prompted, indicate that you'd like to install Microsoft Reader. Follow the instructions to install the program and be sure to visit the activation web page to activate your Pocket PC so that Microsoft Reader will function.

Killer Tip   *Microsoft Reader is not the only e-book application available for the Pocket PC. Another service, called MobiPocket, is also phenomenally popular. It uses its own custom e-book reader to give you access to a wealth of e-books that are available exclusively from www.mobipocket.com.*

There are dozens of online sources for e-books, both free and commercial. Free books are usually from the public domain: either their copyrights have expired (as in the case of classic literature) or they've been written and released by authors not seeking compensation. There are literally thousands of titles available in the public domain.

Commercial titles aren't unlike what you'd buy in a bookstore: they've simply been converted to some electronic format and authorized for sale online. When you buy one, you're effectively buying a license to read it on your Pocket PC and only your Pocket PC.

The first place you might want to look is Microsoft's own web site for Microsoft Reader, www.microsoft.com/reader. This site lists many popular e-book resources, like www.amazon.com, www.fictionwise.com, and www.ebooks.com (see Figure 3-2).

At these sites, you will find thousands of texts in a wide array of categories such as business, history, travel, biography, sci-fi, and classics. Whether you're looking for a collection of Mexican recipes, a Zane Grey western, a sappy love poem, or a classic work by Dickens, you'll be able to find almost anything in e-book format—and best of all, you can carry several books on your PDA at once and your device never gets fatter or heavier. It's a great solution for the bookworm in all of us.

FIGURE 3-2 Thanks to e-books, now you can buy bestsellers online and read them moments later—no need to visit the bookstore.

FIND IT ON THE CD
Microsoft Reader, Free
Microsoft
www.microsoft.com/reader

28 ReaderWorks Standard

Create an E-Book

It has been said that the new Information Age we live in is a great leveler—it has made it possible for anyone to write the Great American Novel (or the Great Norwegian Novel or the Great Kuwaiti Novel) and get it read by a huge audience. While it's true that most of us still read stuff written by a few dozen modern literary giants by buying paperbacks in the bookstore, e-books are indeed making it possible for you to publish and distribute your own literature with an ease that Guttenberg never would have anticipated.

Suppose you indeed have a book you've slaved over for a decade and you're finally ready to show it to friends and family. Since they all have Pocket PCs, why not give it to them as an e-book? Heck, you can put all sorts of things on your PDA in e-book form; it doesn't have to be a depressing story about the Great Depression. But how?

There are a number of e-book creation programs out there, but why not start with something that's free? ReaderWorks Standard is on the CD, and it'll turn any Microsoft Word document into an e-book. Let's make an e-book:

1. Start with a single-spaced Word document. You should also set the font fairly small; a font size of 10 is a good starting place. If you want to divide the book into chapters, use Word's Bookmark feature to tag all the individual chapter breaks.

2. Now it's time to open ReaderWorks. Click the Source Files button on the left side of the screen and then use the Add button to designate your Word file as the source for your e-book.

3. Click Properties. You can fill out as many or as few of these "tags" as you like, to identify the author, subject, description, and so on.

4. Click Table of Contents. This is an optional setting, but if you want your e-book to be browsable by chapter (and if you used the Word Bookmark feature), here's where you set it up. Click the TOC Wizard button and, in the Table of Contents Wizard dialog box, click Next. On the next page, select only the third option,

Extract Bookmarks from Word Source Files. Click Next two more times to build the TOC, then click Finish when the TOC is complete.

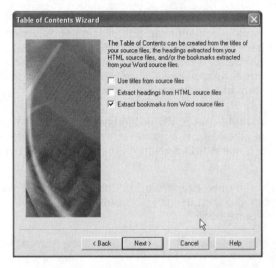

5. You're almost done. Click the Build eBook button at the top of the window (it has multicolored gears in it). If you want to easily e-mail the file to other Pocket PC users, select the option to Build eBook to Microsoft Reader on This Computer. Create the e-book, and then you can e-mail it from your PC. To read the book on your own Pocket PC, drag and drop it to your Pocket PC's My Documents folder. If you'd rather send it directly to your Pocket PC, choose the first option (Reading Device Using Synchronized Files) and create the e-book.

After all that hard work—or at least five minutes of effort—here's the e-book on a Pocket PC:

FIND IT ON THE CD
ReaderWorks Standard, Free
OverDrive
www.overdrive.com

29 Total Remote
Control Your TV

Ever since people began accessorizing their living rooms with multiple home entertainment devices—TVs, stereo receivers, CD players, VCRs, DVD players—folks have cringed at the inevitable farm of remote controls and tried to consolidate everything into a single device. A single universal remote allows you to operate every device in your home theater. Gone is the clutter of a shoebox full of remotes. Gone are the problems associated with remembering how to operate five different gadgets. No more swapping remotes just to change channels and adjust the volume. And most importantly, your significant other can finally master how to turn on the television, set it to Dolby Digital, and play a DVD without your help.

Universal remotes are expensive, though. Really good ones—not the cheap blister-packed models from Wal-Mart—tend to cost hundreds or (hold on to your hat) thousands of dollars. But PDAs have infrared ports. Could your Pocket PC be transformed into a universal remote?

Yes, indeed. There are a handful of remote control applications for the Pocket PC that let you use your favorite PDA to operate your TV, VCR, DVD player, and more.

We're quite fond of Total Remote, a program from Griffin Technology. Total Remote, as you can see below, allows your Pocket PC to function as a universal remote for all of your home entertainment gadgets. The program is easy to configure because it comes with profiles for over 300 devices like TVs, VCRs, DVDs, and more. To add a device to your list of gadgets, choose Device | Active Devices and choose one from the list of gadgets that have profiles.

Can't find your A/V receiver or VCR on the list? You can also make your own device profiles. Choose Device | New and name your gadget; then use the Edit menu to teach your Pocket PC commands from older remotes. If you do end up teaching Total Remote how to work button by button, you'll find it's easier to do than on most remote control programs—you can rotate the screen 180 degrees when in learn mode, so both remotes point the same way. (To do that, choose Tools | Options and select Rotate Screen When Sampling.)

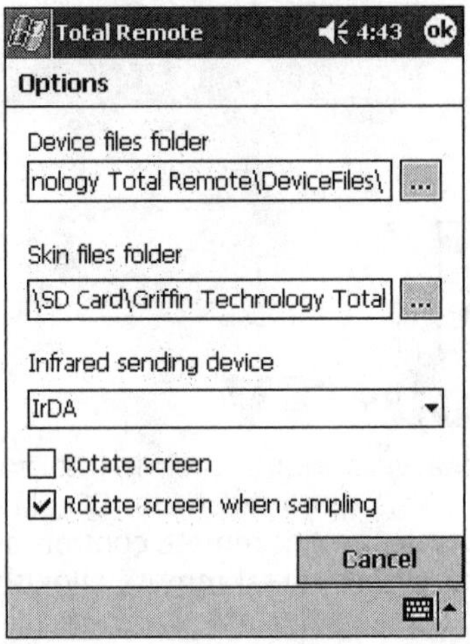

If you like Total Remote, you should know that you'll get even better performance by plugging an infrared extender—called the Remote Transmitter Module—into the headphone jack of your Pocket PC. Griffin claims that you can extend the range of your Pocket PC to a hundred feet, which should make it more than powerful enough to work in any living room (unless you happen to be *The Simpsons'* C. Montgomery Burns).

FIND IT ON THE CD
Total Remote, $24.99
Griffin Technology
www.griffintechnology.com

30 PocketTV

A Tiny Little Movie Theater in Your Pocket

Nothing says "futuristic" quite like watching a movie on your Pocket PC. On a recent cross-country flight, for instance, Dave watched an episode of the short-lived Fox Sci-fi series *Jake 2.0* on his PDA. "What's that?" asked a nearby passenger. "Are you really watching a movie?" After explaining that, indeed, you can easily install video from television, DVD, videotape, or the Internet onto a Pocket PC, she looked utterly amazed. "I use mine for my appointments, and I sometimes play Bejeweled," she confided. "I wish I could do that."

Well, she can. And so can you.

It stands to reason that you'll need some sort of video player on your PDA in order to watch a movie. Of course, you get the Windows Media Player right in the box, which can show any movie in Windows Media (WMV) format without any additional steps. Just copy the movie file to the Pocket PC's system memory or, more likely, an expansion card (movies tend to be quite large and none but the very shortest of clips will fit in a device's internal memory), and go. But keep in mind that there's a lot more content out there in other formats, though—especially MPEG—so you might want to augment the built-in player with a third-party alternative. We've provided PocketTV on the CD, and suggest that you give it a try. After all, it's free. When you start the program for the first time, you will need to register it (don't worry, that's free), but after that you can drag and drop MPEG files onto your Pocket PC and watch them using the simple PocketTV interface:

 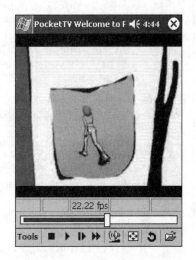

So, suppose you have a movie or two on your computer. Think you're ready to watch video on your next plane trip? Maybe not. In some cases, you might really be ready to kick back and watch *Logan's Run*. But a lot of the time, you still need to convert, compress, and synchronize. Consider this: you download a vintage Throwing Muses music video from Beestung.net. When you inspect the video, though, you find that it's in a format called DIVX—and PocketTV only plays MPEGs. Game over? Nope. You just need to convert the file from DIVX to MPEG.

To do that, you'll need an intermediate utility that lets you save a video file in a different format. For that, you need a conversion utility like EO-Video (www.eo-video.com). EO-Video is a polished, easy-to-use video tool that lets you load files in a broad range of formats and save them as almost anything else. You can load a QuickTime file, for instance, and save it as an MPEG video. Once you've tuned your movie into a file format that your Pocket PC can understand, just copy it to the PDA and you're ready to kick back to video on the really small screen.

Finding Movies for Your PDA

Having a video player on your PDA is all well and good, but it's a lot like being all dressed up with nowhere to go: where do you get the movies for your PDA to begin with?

The reality is that you have an embarrassment of riches when it comes to sources for video. People who watch movies on their PDAs can draw on television and videotape, DVD, their digital camcorder, and even the Internet.

■ Television—whether live, off the air, or stored on videotape—is a common source of video for your PDA. You might want to copy this week's episode of *Friends* or *24* to a Pocket PC, for instance, so you can watch it when you travel. In order for this to work, you'll need some mechanism on your computer, like a composite-video-in or S-Video input, to capture analog video and store it on your PC. Some multimedia computers ship with video capture capabilities. If your computer doesn't already have one, you can add an ATI All-in-Wonder card to your PC, which has video inputs and the necessary software to store video on a hard disk. Another alternative: Dazzle's Digital Video Creator is a USB media hub that sits outside your PC and lets you capture video onto your PC via composite video or S-Video ports.

■ Digital video is getting very popular as well. To get digital video, from a DV or Digital8 camcorder, onto your computer takes a FireWire port (also known as IEEE 1394 or i.Link). Many computers come with at least one FireWire connection, but if yours doesn't, you can add one for under $100. Just fire up your video editing software (which often comes with your camcorder) and capture your movie on the computer's hard drive. When you're done, you may need to save or export the video in a different file format.

■ DVD is the way most of us watch our movies these days, so it stands to reason that we'd want to be able to copy DVD to PDA. PDQ. Suppose you just rented *My Big Fat Greek Wedding* but you're going out of town before you have a chance to watch it. If you copy it to your Pocket PC, you can watch it in stolen moments during your trip. The problem, of course, is getting the movie off of the silver platter and onto your computer's hard disk. Since DVDs are so well copy-protected, this might initially seem like a hopeless task. Fret not—there are several programs around that make this possible. Programs like DVD-to-AVI (www.dvd-to-avi.com) and MovieJack (www.moviejack.org) can "rip" the content from DVD and store the movie as an AVI or MPEG file on your computer's hard drive. From there, it's a matter of synchronizing the movie with your PDA. And then there's DVD to Pocket PC (www.makayama.com), but when we wrote this chapter the program was not intended for U.S. users due to copyright concerns.

■ The Internet is teeming with movies and television shows, if you know where to look. Peer-to-peer services like Kazaa or LimeWire, for instance, have tons of short and long video clips you can download from other people's computers. You can also find web sites dedicated to miniaturized video that's optimized for the small PDA screen. Try www.pocketpcfilms.com, a site that has a few dozen movies for rent—ranging from classic TV programs and old films to sports, self-help, and Adam Sandler films. Want to see some action flicks that show off Clive Owen and BMW cars? Download movies from www.bmwfilms.com. And be sure to check out www.pocketrocketfx.com, www.mp3downloadcenter.com, and www.cinemapop.com.

FIND IT ON THE CD

PocketTV, Free
Pocket TV
www.pockettv.com

31 Pocket Player

Rockin' in Your Pocket

Woo hoo! Rock and roll! Portable digital music players are so common these days that there's nothing particularly magical about them—even when you consider the fact they let you carry dozens or even hundreds of hours of music on the go. But to combine a digital music player and a PDA—now that's something of a revelation. One little pocket-sized gadget holds your contacts, calendar, important documents, and yes, all of your most essential music. Just plug in a pair of headphones and you can read a book on your PDA (check out "Read an E-Book," earlier in this chapter) while grooving to your favorite Throwing Muses album.

And Microsoft makes it easy—Windows Media Player, that same program that plays WMV-format movies, also handles digital music files. Getting music into your PDA is simple, but the exact process depends upon what kind of music you, in fact, own:

■ If you have plain old MP3 files or WMA files that are not copy protected, then copying files is easy. You can insert your Pocket PC's memory card into a desktop USB card reader, and just drag and drop it into the My Documents folder. Or, you can open the Pocket PC on your Windows desktop and drag and drop the files into the My Documents folder. Put the memory card back in your PDA and you're ready to rock.

■ If you have a collection of copy-protected WMA files, you can't just drag and drop. Instead, you need to use the desktop version of Windows Media Player. Make sure that your PDA is in its ActiveSync cradle and turned on. Start Windows Media Player and create a playlist of music you want to copy in the program's Copy to CD or Device tab (see Figure 3-3). Then choose your Pocket PC's memory card from the list on the right side of the screen and click the Copy button. Windows Media Player will then (slowly) copy the songs to your Pocket PC in a playable form, with its license information intact.

Now that you know how to copy music to your PC, you deserve a better music player. Windows Media Player is okay, but it's visually boring and hard to use. We prefer Pocket Player, from Conduits Technology. This program is compatible with a wide

FIGURE 3-3   Windows Media Player can copy tunes to your PDA.

variety of skins that let you change the look of the program, and even the default skin is dramatically more attractive than Windows Media Player:

By default, Pocket Player finds all the music on your Pocket PC, but that may include lots of little WAV file sound effects that you don't want to listen to. To create a playlist, tap the tab on the left of the Now Playing box and you'll see the dialog box from the illustration on the left; to select a single song and listen to it immediately, tap the tab on the right and you'll see the illustration on the right.

Killer Tip   *Tap the musical note button in the middle of the screen to get to the program's options.*

32 Replay Radio

Radio Waves

Remember radio? It was a great little invention in its day, but time has passed that venerable little gadget by. These days, we tend to listen to talk radio shows and even some music over the Internet. Heck, as Dave is sitting at his computer, he's listening to Mike Rosen (the single most articulate, intellectual political commentator on radio today) on 850 KOA (a Denver talk radio station) by sitting at his computer, not in front of a radio. And no matter what your taste—NPR, Rushbo, "Car Talk"—you can tune into the chatter via a desktop audio player.

That's great, but like all important people, we also spend a lot of time on the go, and so we'd like to listen to Mike Rosen's acerbic wit whenever and wherever the mood strikes us. Impossible, you say? Not really. TiVo and Replay long ago proved that you could record TV shows and watch them at your leisure; now a program called Replay Radio does the same for radio. And that means you can easily take your radio on the road.

Replay Radio, from Applian (www.applian.com; see Figure 3-4), is almost too cool for words. We've put a trial copy on the CD so you can see for yourself. Like a TiVo for Internet radio, it makes recording your favorite radio shows an effortless affair.

To record a show, just click Add Show and fill in the dialog box. You'll need to use the Pick a Show or Pick a Station buttons at the top of the dialog box, or you can enter any URL you find on the Web if the show you want isn't already listed. The program comes equipped with about 120 or so preset national shows—everything from *Gordon Liddy* to *Meet the Press* to *Kim Kommando.* Just pick the shows you want to record, set a few details like the bitrate of the MP3 file and the frequency of the recording (Just once? Every day?), then forget it. When you've filled out the details, click OK and you've set up a recurring recording, just like using TiVo.

Once a recording is complete, just install it on your PDA's memory card and away you go. Since it's in standard MP3 format, it will play on your Pocket PC using Windows Media Player or any other digital music player that you prefer. As long as Replay Radio is running in the background of your PC, MP3 files show up in a designated folder, ready for installation on your Pocket PC. We thought we liked Internet radio before, but Replay Radio has turned it into a truly obsessive love affair.

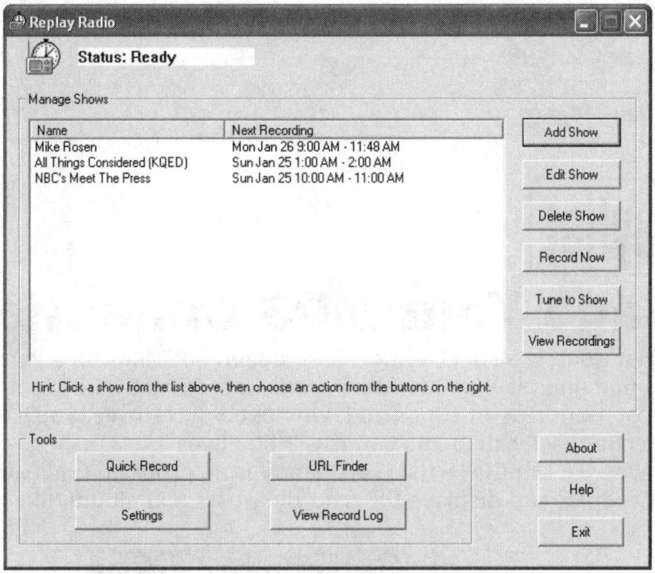

FIGURE 3-4   Replay Radio lets you record any radio show and transfer it to a PDA for playback on the road.

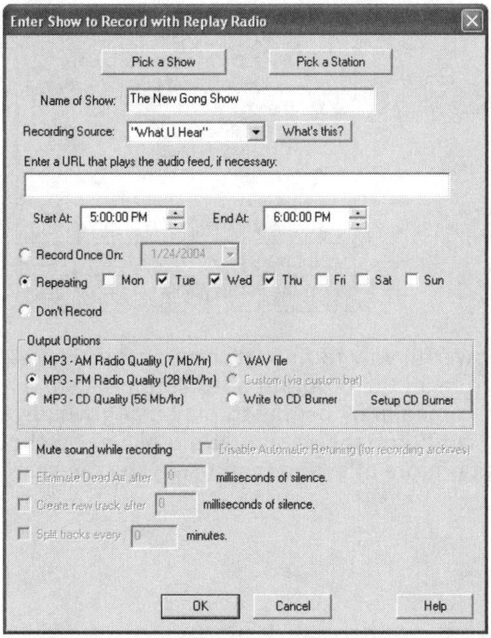

FIGURE 3-5   Configure Replay Radio to record a show once or every day.

FIND IT ON THE CD
Replay Radio, $29.95
Applian
www.replay-radio.com

33 CEPlaylist

Manage Your MP3 Collection

Really—what good is a collection of three dozen MP3 files on a Pocket PC when it's too difficult to find and play just the tracks you want? Slap a 1GB memory card into your PDA and load hundreds of songs and, we hope you can see, you'll lose control of your music collection faster than you can say "Abba lives."

That's why we like CEPlaylist. This handy little program finds all of the digital music on your Pocket PC and displays the data by artists and album, like this:

It's a clever, powerful way to find your music quickly and effectively.

But that's far from all the program does. Tap on a song and then tap the Play button—the song immediately begins to play using whatever your preferred music player is (you can configure the default audio player by choosing File | Player from the menu). That's far more effective than using the file search tools in most Pocket PC music players.

But we saved the best for last. You can build custom playlists with CEPlaylist (hence, we suppose, the name). To do that, follow these steps:

1. Choose File | New Playlist from the menu.

2. Tap the Song Library tab at the bottom of the screen.

3. Tap a song that you want to add to your new playlist. Then tap the button that has an arrow popping out of a musical note. The song has been added to the playlist.

4. Continue adding songs to the playlist in this way.

5. Check up on your playlist by tapping the Song List tab. Here you can see all the songs you've added:

6. When you're done, choose File | Save As and give your playlist a name.

Your new playlist will be available in any music player on your Pocket PC. If you prefer, you can even start the playlist from CEPlaylist—go to the Playlists tab, check the playlist you want to play, and then tap the Play button at the bottom of the screen. The playlist will launch in your favorite audio player!

FIND IT ON THE CD
CEPlaylist, $9.95
Creative Engineering
www.ceng.com

34 Wine Enthusiast Guide

Pick the Perfect Wine

There are few tasks in the world more onerous than selecting a wine. On the way to a party, you stop in the store and are immediately overwhelmed by enough French language and pretentious salespeople to make you want to grab a six-pack of Coke instead. Wouldn't it be great if you could bring a team of wine shopping experts with you whenever you needed to make such a decision? You can, sort of—if you have a wine reference guide on your PDA.

We like the LandWare Wine Enthusiast Guide. It was created by *Wine Enthusiast Magazine* and features an exhaustive guide to selecting wines along with the ability to track and manage your own wine collection. There's even a glossary of wine terminology—handy if you don't know your Abboccato from your Barbera.

When you start the program and see the main Buying Guide screen, notice the Wine Selector button at the bottom right:

Tap it to launch the Wine Selector Wizard, which lets you choose the right wine for your occasion. You can customize a price and quality of wine, then choose a style (like red, white, or dessert wine), the grape variety (the program's built-in glossary may come in handy for this tool), and even the region from which the wine is derived.

When you're done, tap OK to see your potential wine candidates.

Finally, check out the statistics for each wine. When you find a wine you are interested in, tap on it. You'll see a screen like this, which gives you lots of information about the selected wine:

FIND IT ON THE CD
Wine Enthusiast Guide, $19.95
LandWare
www.landware.com

---

35 BarBack Drink Guide
Mix the Perfect Drink

Do you like to imagine that you're Tom Cruise from the classic movie *Cocktail?* Or maybe, like Rick, you see yourself as Piper Perabo from *Coyote Ugly* (he even wears high heels when he mixes drinks around the house). Let's put it this way: even if you don't fantasize about being the hero in a bartender movie, you might still want to know how to mix up some drinks. And while Bart Simpson could follow the recipes behind the bar while mixing drinks for the Mafia, you may not have that advantage. Instead, rely on your Pocket PC to help you make your drinks.

The BarBack Drink Guide, from Town Compass, is a superb reference for making just about any kind of drink imaginable. BarBack includes 10,000 different drinks. The main screen lets you select the kind of drink category:

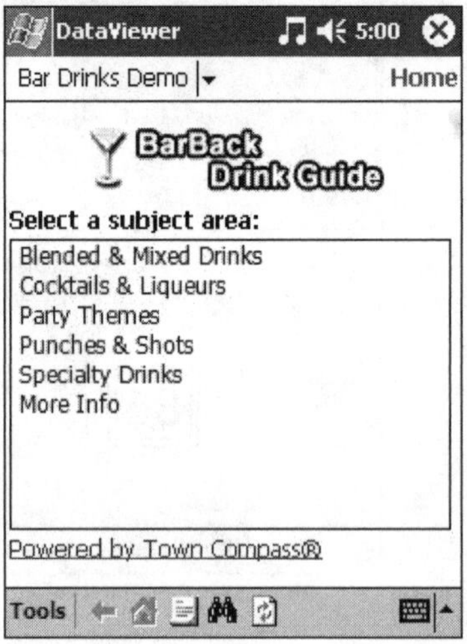

From there, you can fine-tune your drink from the resulting drop-down box:

And finally, you can see a complete list of all the drinks in that category. When you find the drink you like, tap it for a complete recipe. The recipe even tells you what kind of glass to use for the most authentic look.

FIND IT ON THE CD

BarBack Drink Guide, $9.95
Town Compass
www.pocketdirectory.com

36 MoviesCE

Choose the Perfect Movie

Seen any good movies lately? Your chances may improve with the right software on your PDA. Instead of wandering aimlessly through the local DVD rental store and hoping you make the right choice (our advice: avoid any three-word movie titles, like Tough to Kill, Ready to Die, or Pining for Revenge), we suggest trying a program like MoviesCE.

MoviesCE is a movie database that holds tons of information about movies you have seen and plan to see:

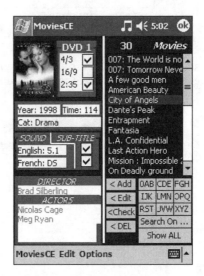

The full version of the program (not the demo included on this CD) comes with about 350 movies in total. The demo, on the other hand, has a "starter" collection of about three dozen titles. Tap on a movie that looks interesting, and you'll be privy to the DVD's cover art, aspect ratio of the film, running time, cast information, and more.

The program lets you cross-reference details between movies. If you are looking at *Dante's Peak,* for instance, and think, "Gee, I don't want to see this movie, but now that I think about it, I'd like to see something else with Pierce Brosnan," you're in luck. Just tap the actor's name and Movies CE will immediately search its database for other titles with that actor. To return to the entire list of movies, tap the Show All button at the bottom right of the screen.

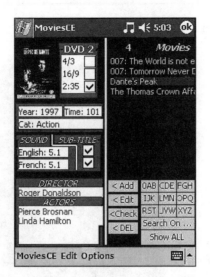

You can add new movies to the database, but you'll need the full version to do that—the demo is read-only.

FIND IT ON THE CD

MoviesCE, $19.95
Patrice Pennetier
www.pocketpc.pennetier.com

37 Pocket Stars

Follow the Stars

"My God," David Bowman said in *2001: A Space Odyssey*, "It's full of stars." While he was referring to the black, rectangular monolith that was orbiting Jupiter, the same can be said of your Pocket PC—with the right software. Using a star chart application like Pocket Stars, from Nomad Electronics, you can put a planetarium in your pocket and reference it anywhere, anytime—at home, at work, or when you're hauling the telescope into the backyard.

This is truly one of the most impressive programs you'll ever find for the Pocket PC and one that you can pull out when someone wants to know "what else that organizer can do." When you first start the program, it displays the stars and planets visible directly overhead at the current time, based on the Pocket PC's clock. You can also pan around the display by dragging the stylus and zoom in and out by using the magnifying glasses at the bottom of the screen:

Of course, Pocket Stars may not know exactly where you are. To configure the program, tap the globe icon at the bottom right of the screen and choose the LatLong tab. Choose your city from the list, pick the approximate location from the map, or enter a latitude and longitude directly.

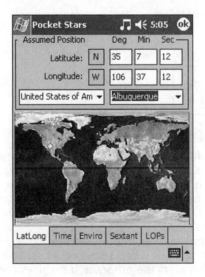

Pocket Stars is a great astronomy resource. To find more information about any object in the sky, tap it for a brief summary in the upper-left corner of the screen, or tap and hold, then choose Info from the menu for a full-screen encyclopedia-like entry.

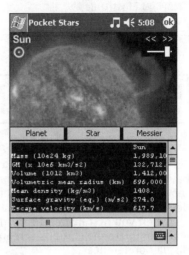

One of our favorite features is the animation mode. Tap the clock icon at the bottom of the screen to step through the night sky at a far accelerated rate—in hourly, daily, monthly, or even annual increments. This mode often looks best when you turn on the orbital paths, so you can graphically see the way objects move through the sky. To do that, tap the A and select Orbital Paths from the View options.

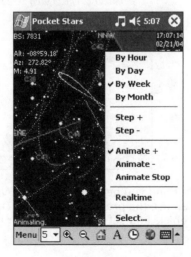

FIND IT ON THE CD
Pocket Stars, $19.95
Nomad Electronics
www.nomadelectronics.com

38 Personal Vehicle Manager

Manage Your Motorcoach

Do you meticulously track every detail of your car's maintenance? Then you should have a program like Personal Vehicle Manager on your Pocket PC. It'll let you stay on top of maintenance, repairs, and fuelings without needing to remember to jot down details when you get home—because you can record it all when it happens.

When you first install the program, Personal Vehicle Manager needs to get to know you. Complete the Options screen so the program uses the right kinds of units and display preferences.

From there, the first thing you need to do is add a vehicle. The program manages multiple cars, so you can use the program to keep track of all the vehicles in your family. Choose New | Vehicle and set it up with the car name, odometer reading, and other details.

```
┌─────────────────────────────────────┐
│ 🪟 Personal Vehicle Ma 🎵 ◀ 5:11  ok │
├─────────────────────────────────────┤
│ Fuel Entry (Nissan 350Z Roadster '04) │
│                                       │
│         Date: │Sat , Jan 24, 2004  ▼│ │
│                                       │
│    Odometer: │25588        │⬍│        │
│                                       │
│   No. of gal: │11.4    │⬍│ ┐ Enter any 2 │
│                            │ values and │
│ Price per gal: │1.91   │⬍│ ┤ click Compute │
│                            │            │
│   Total Cost: │21.77   │⬍│ ┘ │Compute│ │
│                                       │
│                                       │
│                                       │
│                                       │
│                                       │
│  Details │ Vendor │ Notes │           │
├─────────────────────────────────────┤
│ ⊗ Cancel                      ⌨ ▲    │
└─────────────────────────────────────┘
```

Once you have a car entered into the system, using the program is simply a matter of selecting that car and then choosing whatever data you want to enter from the New menu.

Our favorite tool in this program is the fuel efficiency tracker. After all, the health of your car is easily measured by its fuel efficiency—if you notice a sudden drop in fuel performance, that may signal a major problem with your car. But you can't tell unless you're actively tracking fuel efficiency all the time. Try this: tap the fuel pump icon at the bottom of the screen and enter your fuel data the next time you stop for gas. Complete the Fuel Entry form and tap OK. As long as you keep the odometer readings up-to-date each time you visit the gas station, you can tap the Quick Stats icon at the bottom of the screen at any time to find the fuel efficiency of the car—along with other pertinent information.

```
┌─────────────────────────────────────┐
│ 🪟 Personal Vehicle Ma 🎵 ◀ 5:11  ok │
├─────────────────────────────────────┤
│ Quick Stats. (Nissan 350Z Roadster '04) │
├─────────────────────────────────────┤
│ Date Range: <All Dates>               │
│ Fuel economy (avg): 26.25 mi/gal      │
│ Fuel economy (last): 25.26 mi/gal     │
│   Distance travelled: 588 mi          │
│      Fuel consumed: 22.40 gal         │
│    Fuel consumed @: 3.81 gal per 100 mi │
│   Cost of ownership: $12.96 per 100 mi │
│ Upcoming Maintenance:                 │
│ (due within the next 2 weeks or 500 mi.) │
│ ┌──────┬───────┬──────────────┐       │
│ │ Due ...│ Odmtr.│ Description  │      │
│ ├──────┴───────┴──────────────┤       │
│ │                              │       │
│ │                              │       │
│ │                              │       │
│ └──────────────────────────────┘      │
├─────────────────────────────────────┤
│ Alt. Units                    ⌨ ▲    │
└─────────────────────────────────────┘
```

FIND IT ON THE CD
Personal Vehicle Manager, $19.95
Two Peaks Software
www.twopeaks.com

39 Diet & Exercise Assistant

Lose Weight and Get in Shape

Dieting and watching what you eat is hard work. You might have a plan, but it's at home...and here you are on your lunch break. What to do? If you're like Rick, you'll just assume that Twinkies are nutritious and hope for the best.

But if you're like Dave, you'll try the Diet & Exercise Assistant for Pocket PC.

This program is a comprehensive weight and nutrition monitoring system for your Pocket PC. You begin by inputting your personal information (such as height, weight, age, and gender), and the software automatically calculates the calories you burn during the day. Then you build on that foundation by setting a weight loss goal—how much weight you intend to lose and a target date for making that happen. The program lets you monitor your progress with charts and graphs while a calorie calculator automatically calculates the number of calories you need to remove from your diet in order to achieve your weight loss goal.

Diet & Exercise ♫ ◀€ 5:14 ok	Diet & Exercise ♫ ◀€ 5:14 ok
◀ ▦ ▶ Saturday January 24, 2004	Set Weight Goals ▾
Weight: 188 lbs [Weight]	Goals
Meals: 0 cal [Meals]	Start: 188 lbs
BMR: 2262 cal [BMR]	Saturday January 24, 2004 [Set]
Exercise: 0 cal [Exercise]	Goal: 175 lbs
Total: -2262 cal Water: 0 ▲▼	Monday March 1, 2004 [Set]
Goal: -1229 cal	Calorie Calculator
Food Budget: 1033 cal	To lose 13 lbs in 37 days, you will need to eat 1229 fewer calories per day than your body burns.
📄 ⊕ ⬚ ◆ ▦ ▨ ✉ ▦ ▲	
Record Edit Options ⌨▲	Goals Options ⚠ ⌨▲

The program has a huge food database with over 8,000 food items—you can use this master menu to build your own diet plan. The program then tracks your nutrition by monitoring calories, carbohydrates, protein, fiber, fat, and saturated fat.

The other half of any diet, of course, is exercise. The Diet & Exercise Assistant tracks your exercise activities from a large exercise database. Simply input the minutes you spend exercising, and the software automatically calculates the calories you burned through exercise. If an exercise is not in the database, you can optionally log your own user-defined exercises.

FIND IT ON THE CD

Diet & Exercise Assistant, $19.95
Keyoe, Inc.
www.keyoe.com

Chapter

Fun and Games

All work and no play makes, well, Dave. But there's nothing dull about your PDA, which is capable of some truly excellent fun. This includes not only practical fun, like the golf scorecard program that kicks off this chapter, but also classic boardgames like Monopoly, classic computer games like SimCity, and classic parlor games like pool. Whether you've got five minutes to kill while waiting for a taxi or five hours on a coast-to-coast flight, you'll find plenty of entertainment on your PDA.

40 IntelliGolf

To the Links, Caddie!

Rick is not a golfer. Dave is not a golfer. So you're probably thinking, "Right, like I'm going to take golf advice from two guys who don't know a sand wedge from a sandwich." Hey, it's okay with us if you don't try IntelliGolf—but you'll be missing out on the coolest scorecard program in all of recorded golf history (which goes back more than *ten* years!).

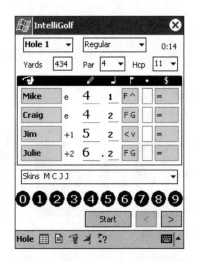

Calling IntelliGolf a scorecard program belies its capabilities. While it can indeed keep score for up to five players per round, it can also track shots for every club, manage wagering games (such as skins, scramble, and point quota), and show you statistics and graphs based on your performance over time. It also enables you to download course information—hole par, handicap, and length—for over 18,000 courses, so you don't have to input all that stuff manually before your round. Just download the course from the IntelliGolf web site, ActiveSync your PDA, and hit the links.

The Birdie Edition of IntelliGolf includes a Windows component (see Figure 4-1) that synchronizes with your PDA and gives you a more complete overview of your rounds, statistics, and so on. You can also print your scorecards and post them around the office for bragging rights (or some good-natured ribbing—"Look, Dave shot a 397!").

Date	Score	Course	Players
4/3/2002	93	Vicwood Golf Links	HR Warren, Jack Elliott, Greg Elliot, Mike Patterson
3/27/2002	105	Vicwood Golf Links	John Randal, Brian Pearson, Doug Mack
2/10/2002	103	Desert Canyon	John Randal, Mark Taylor, Fred Cox III
8/1/2001	104	Apple Mountain Golf Resort	John Randal, Chris Mack, Pete
7/31/2001	108	Turkey Creek Golf Club	John Randal, Chris Mack, Player 3, John

Player: John Randal   Show: Scores, notes, and games   Start: 10:07 AM   Finish: 2:48 PM

HOLE	1	2	3	4	5	6	7	8	9	OUT	10	11	12	13	14	15	16	17
White	337	496	126	359	395	154	394	385	519	3165	369	321	518	160	398	376	153	347
John Randal	4	9	5	4	7	5	5	6	9	54	5	6	6	3	6	7	4	6
Brian Pearson	5	5	4	7	6	4	4	5	5	45	6	6	5	4	5	5	4	4
Doug Mack	5	6	5	4	5	3	5	6	6	45	5	5	5	4	7	5	4	6
PAR	4	5	3	4	4	3	4	4	5	36	4	4	5	3	4	4	3	4
HANDICAP	15	9	17	11	1	13	5	3	7		10	16	4	18	8	2	12	14
Fairways hit	x	>		<			x	x	<	3	x		x					>
Greens in reg.							x			1				x			x	

29 Rounds   C:\Program Files\IntelliGolf\golf.gdb

FIGURE 4-1 When you ActiveSync, IntelliGolf Birdie Edition transfers all the details of your round from your PDA to your PC, where you can track your progress, print scorecards, and more.

Killer Tip *If you don't need or want the Windows component, you can save $10 by purchasing IntelliGolf Par Edition, which includes only the Pocket PC software. All the other features are the same, and your data still gets backed up when you ActiveSync.*

The latest version of IntelliGolf has one particularly advanced feature that merits attention. If you have a GPS receiver that works with your PDA, IntelliGolf can compute the exact distance from your location on the fairway to the green. Armed with that information, you can select the best club for your shot and, hopefully, shave some strokes from your score.

To use this IntelliGPS technology, you need two things: a GPS receiver that's compatible with your PDA, and GPS coordinates for the course you're playing. The latter are included with the course info you download from the IntelliGolf web site, though not all courses have been updated with the necessary GPS data. For those that aren't, you can record the coordinates yourself during your first round of play—then you'll have them for all future rounds.

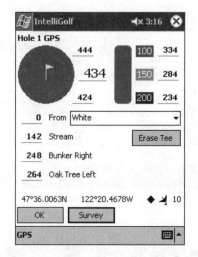

As for the GPS receiver, there are countless choices. If your PDA has a built-in (or even add-on) Bluetooth radio, your best bet is a Bluetooth GPS. That's because it's wireless, meaning you could leave the receiver strapped to your golf bag and still obtain coordinates on your PDA from up to 30 feet away. ALK, Belkin, Delorme, and Socket are among the GPS companies that offer Bluetooth receivers. They also offer wired solutions for non-Bluetooth PDAs.

FIND IT ON THE CD
IntelliGolf 7.0 Birdie Edition, $39.95
Karrier Communications
www.IntelliGolf.com

41 SimCity

Manage Your Own City

Dave's definition of a fun game is one in which things "blow up real good." Rick prefers thinking to carnage, hence his fondness for SimCity 2000—a thinking person's game in the truest sense. You've probably heard of the eponymous desktop classic, which in the late '80s just about ruined personal productivity with its highly addictive mix of city building and management. (City building and management? Sounds about as much fun as a root canal, but trust us when we say it's thoroughly engaging. It wouldn't be a classic otherwise.)

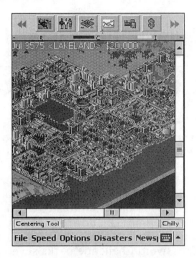

SimCity 2000 for Pocket PC is a licensed version of the original, meaning it looks and plays exactly the same. You start with an empty stretch of land; it's up to you to build roads, power plants, residential areas, police and fire departments, and so on. In other words, you're pretty much a deity. Once teeny little sim-citizens start moving into your mini-metropolis, you shift gears from god to mayor (same difference), working overtime to keep everyone happy. That means keeping taxes low while still generating enough revenue for new roads, more power plants, the occasional football stadium—get the idea?

Killer Tip *If you just can't make ends meet and don't mind a little harmless cheating, type **imacheat** using the onscreen keyboard. You'll instantly get an extra $500,000 in your city's coffers. Want to see a nuclear meltdown? Type **buddamus**. Start a fire? Type **mrsoleary**.*

If things are humming along nicely (or even if they're not), you can put on the god shoes again and see how your city deals with a "natural" disaster: fire, flood, and maybe a visit from good old Godzilla. Mwa ha ha ha! (Don't be afraid to indulge your god complex—you can always rebuild after a catastrophe.)

All this should come as good news to SimCity fans (and simulation fans in general). Now for the bad news. Because the game has to squish into your PDA's relatively small screen, you don't get to see as much of your city at a time, so you wind up scrolling around quite a bit—which kills some of the fun. Even so, SimCity 2000 looks great and remains just as fun today as it was a decade ago.

FIND IT ON THE CD
SimCity 2000, $29.95
Zio Interactive
www.ziointeractive.com

42 Merriam-Webster Crossword Challenge

Big Book of Crosswords—In Your Little PDA

POWER APP

One of the reasons we're so fond of reading books on our PDAs (see Chapter 3) is convenience: it's a lot easier to fit a PDA in your pocket than a copy of Stephen King's latest hardcover. Same goes for crossword puzzles: we love doing them, but who wants to carry around a big book of 'em? (Sure, there's always the newspaper, but it gives you just one puzzle, and then you wind up with ink on your fingers, plus they're impossible to open when you're packed into a coach seat, and there's never a pen around when you need one...sigh. Oh, don't get us wrong, we love newspapers, especially ones with Dave Barry, but...where were we?)

Merriam-Webster Crossword Challenge packs several hundred puzzles into your PDA and wraps them in an attractive, easy-to-use interface. Tap any square to see the "across" clue for that word; tap it again to see the "down" clue. You enter letters using an in-game keyboard, not the same one you use to enter other data.

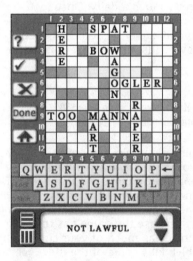

The game lets you play at three different skill levels. The puzzles themselves don't change; rather, each level includes a different number of hints (tap the question-mark icon to reveal the highlighted letter) and "verifies" (used to see if the letter in the selected square is correct—if not, it gets erased). The Easy level gives you ten verifies and five hints, Medium gives you five verifies and three hints, and Hard makes you figure out the puzzle the old-fashioned way.

Killer Tip *We normally advise people to stay away from software that comes on memory cards, as you usually get less than what you pay for. One exception is Mobile Digital Media's Merriam-Webster Crossword Puzzles & Word Challenges (www.gomdm.com), which includes not only Crossword Challenge, but also three other great word games: Link Letters, Text Twist (one of Rick's personal favorites—see "A Game That Boggles the Mind," later in this chapter), and WhatWord. This foursome would cost you about $60 if purchased separately—the card sells for $30 and keeps your PDA's memory free for other stuff. Such a deal!*

Until Crossword Challenge came along, we'd forgotten how much fun crossword puzzles can be. In fact, we'd be remiss if we didn't mention another terrific title: Stand Alone's Crossword Puzzles for Pocket PC (www.standalone.com). It costs $5 more than Crossword Challenge, but it has one important additional feature: it works with puzzles you can download from newspaper web sites across the country. Thus, you not only get a bunch of crosswords from the guy who writes them for the *Washington Post*, you get access to a virtually unlimited supply of extras. Check out the demo—it's on the CD!

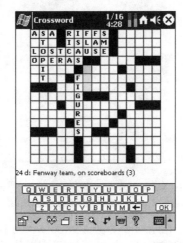

FIND IT ON THE CD
Merriam-Webster Crossword Challenge, $14.95
Hexacto
www.hexacto.com

Find More Software Online

This book is just the tip of the proverbial iceberg. There are thousands of programs available for Pocket PC handhelds, and many of them can be found at Handango (www.handango.com). This site sells Pocket PC software directly, meaning you use a credit card to pay for a program, download it to your PC, and then install it on your PDA. We also recommend visiting PocketGear (www.pocketgear.com), another vast repository of Pocket PC software. If you're looking for something that's not in this book (impossible, we know!), you're likely to find it at one of these two online stores.

43 The Emperor's Mahjong

Can't We All Just Get Mahjong?

The traditional game of mahjong is played with four people seated around a square table, with dozens of ceramic tiles in the middle. Okay, how do you turn that into something you play on your PDA? In the case of The Emperor's Mahjong, you change the rules a bit. (Hey, he's the Emperor, he can do what he wants!)

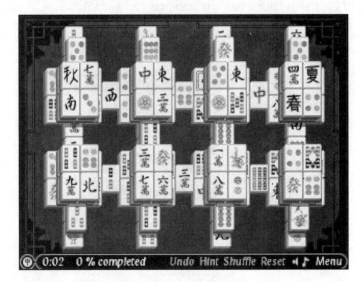

The game works like this: you're presented with a board containing dozens of tiles. You have six minutes in which to clear at least 100 tiles from the board, which is done by tapping identical pairs (or pairs belonging to like families). Needless to say, this is a bit different from traditional mahjong, which has more in common with gin rummy.

Okay, so maybe the Emperor had a little too much sake in classifying this a mahjong game. It's still pretty fun—try the demo and see for yourself.

Killer Tip *Interested in a more traditional mahjong game? Check out Four Winds Mah Jong (www.4windsmj.com), in which you play against three computer opponents and utilize standard mahjong rules. Try the demo—it's on the CD!*

FIND IT ON THE CD
The Emperor's Mahjong, $14.95
Hexacto
www.hexacto.com

44 Trivial Pursuit

Honey, I Shrunk Trivial Pursuit!

Most people have a love/hate relationship with Trivial Pursuit, the 1980s trivia game that once and for all separated the smart people from, well, Dave. Actually, Rick's no champ when it comes to trivia, either, but he'll blow you off the tennis court, so there.

Handmark's Trivial Pursuit re-creates the beloved game on your PDA, allowing you to play it anywhere, anytime, with up to five other players. This version includes over 1,600 multiple-choice and true-false questions (some covering very recent events, such as the SARS epidemic) in six familiar categories: Arts and Entertainment, History, Sports and Leisure, Science and Nature, People and Places, and Wildcard. The goal remains the same: answer questions correctly to fill your game piece with wedges and prove you're the smartest one in the group.

If you'd rather dispense with the game board and just test your trivia knowledge, Trivial Pursuit offers a Flash mode in which you answer questions in order to move up the rungs of a ladder. The first player to reach the top and answer the final question correctly wins the game. Regardless of which mode you choose, Trivial Pursuit serves up the occasional "trivia fact," an informative bit of info related to the question you just answered.

Killer Tip   *Tap the magnifying-glass icon to zoom in on the game board. Tap it again to zoom out and see the entire board. Tap the little dancing-i icons to see additional gameplay tips.*

FIND IT ON THE CD
Trivial Pursuit, $29.99
Handmark
www.handmark.com

45 Battleship, Scrabble, and Yahtzee

Scrabble, Yahtzee, Battleship—It's Like the '70s All Over Again

Back in the '70s, cable TV didn't exist, VCRs were an expensive luxury item, and the Internet wasn't even known as the Internet. (It was called the Arpanet, and it was used primarily to connect government and university mainframe computers. There's your trivia for the day.) Small wonder boardgames were so popular—there was nothing else to do!

Fortunately, many of these games are just as fun today as they were decades ago—and now you don't need a kitchen table (or even other players) to play them. Classics like Scrabble, Yahtzee, and Battleship are available for your PDA, and they're not just clones, either—they're licensed versions of the originals, so they look and play just like you remember. Take a look:

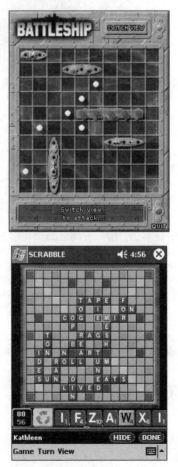

You can play any of these games solo (with one or more computer opponents, depending on the game) or with other people. In fact, all three games support play via infrared, meaning if you have, say, Battleship on your PDA and you're sitting across from someone who has Battleship on his PDA, you can play head-to-head on your respective devices. After you complete your turn, you tap a button to beam your move to the other person, where it's reflected on his screen. He makes his move, beams it to you, and so the game progresses. Of course, you can also take turns on the same PDA—it's just not as cool and geeky.

Killer Tip   *These three games are great diversions for kids old enough to understand the rules. Each one requires at least a little bit of brain power (Scrabble in particular), as opposed to the usual blast-everything-in-sight games kids usually play. And because they're fun for adults as well, they're ideal for the whole family. This message brought to you by Parker Brothers. (Just kidding.)*

FIND IT ON THE CD

Battleship, $19.99
Scrabble, $29.99
Yahtzee, $19.99
Handmark
www.handmark.com

46 All Mobile Casino

Get Ready for Vegas, Baby

Hey, is that a casino in your pocket? It is if you're carrying All Mobile Casino in your pocket. This collection of 11 gambling games—American Roulette, European Roulette, Baccarat ("Welcome back, Mr. Bond"), Blackjack, 6:5 Blackjack, Caribbean Poker, Video Poker, Pai Gow Poker, Casino War, Sic Bo (a popular Chinese dice game), and Slots—features beautiful graphics and nifty sound effects. Best of all, you'll never lose more than $15. Let's see Caesar's Palace match that bet!

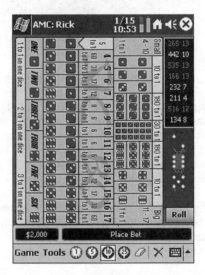

Speaking of Vegas, there's nothing like a little blackjack practice before you hit the tables. All Mobile Casino's version is gorgeous, allowing you to play up to three hands simultaneously from a six-deck chute (perfect for practicing your card counting). It also has a voice feature that announces your card total and says things like "bust" and "blackjack." (If you get tired of the voice feature, turn it off by tapping Tools | Options, then unchecking the Voices box.)

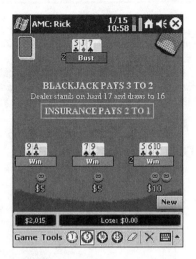

What's interesting about All Mobile Casino is the way it simulates the Vegas experience. At the outset, you create a player and give yourself a monetary stake. This can be as much or as little as you like, but your "virtual wallet" stays with you as you move from one game to another. When you go broke, that's it—you're done. You can always create another player, of course, but having a set limit makes you a more careful gambler—and makes the game seem more realistic. All Mobile Casino also includes built-in help screens for all the games, so fear not if you're not up to speed on the rules of Sic Bo or Pai Gow Poker.

The only lemon in the bunch is slots. All Mobile Casino includes three spiffy-looking machines, but they all seem to have the same problem: you never, ever win. The first slot always comes up the same, and the third one frequently does. Obviously, there's a bug in the software. We've alerted the developers, so hopefully it will be fixed by the time you read this. That's us, always looking out for you, our beloved reader.

Killer Tip *Free Pocket PC games are few and far between, and free ones of the caliber of Drive-Thru Poker (www.portable-games.com) are rare indeed. This polished, colorful video-poker variant stakes you with $100 and gives you 20 hands in which to break the bank or go bust. After you place your bet, you're dealt five cards, any of which can be kept or discarded. You need to end up with at least a pair of jacks to push, better to win. Before you toss your discards, you can halve your bet (if your hand is looking particularly weak) or double it (if it's a strong one). A wild card helps keep things interesting. You can find Drive-Thru Poker on the CD!*

FIND IT ON THE CD
All Mobile Casino, $14.95
BinaryFish
www.binaryfish.com

47 ChessGenius

Hone Your Chess Skills

Whether you're serious about chess or you just enjoy the occasional casual game, there's no better Pocket PC simulation than ChessGenius. The game caters to novices and experts alike and includes 40 different play levels. You can play solo against the computer, play against another person (either on the same PDA or via infrared, assuming your opponent also has ChessGenius installed on his or her PDA), or sit back and watch the computer play itself.

If you're an utter novice like Rick, you'll appreciate ChessGenius's ten beginner levels, in which the game makes deliberate mistakes. It can offer hints regarding your next move and, in Tutor mode, warn you if you've made a bad move. You can even "take it back" and try to make a better move. Once your skills improve, you can switch to the "blitz" levels—timed games in which you have anywhere from 1 to 120 minutes to play the entire match.

Killer Tip *Keep to the center of the board. Occupy it if you can, attack it if your opponent has it. Pawns make excellent soldiers in the war for the center.*

In short, ChessGenius has just about every feature you could want in a chess game, and then some. On the other hand, if you've always found chess a bit dull or slow-moving, have we got an alternative for you. Rook's Revenge (www.astraware.com) presents you with a colorful, but fairly traditional-looking, chess board. Instead of making moves one at a time, your goal is to make them as quickly as possible. You're still limited to the legal moves of each piece, but you don't have to wait for your opponent to make a move before you make your next one. It's like chess on steroids—terrific, addicting, fast-paced fun. Check out the demo on the CD!

FIND IT ON THE CD
ChessGenius, $25
Lang Software
www.chessgenius.com

48 | Backgammon

Ever Wonder Why There's No Frontgammon?

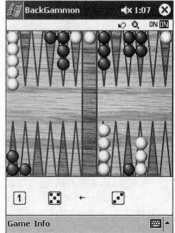

We love backgammon. It's like checkers for grown-ups. Handmark's Backgammon offers just about everything you could want in a PDA version of the game, including one- and two-player competition, a doubling cube, hints and statistics, and a choice of board designs (wooden, marble, and classic).

In case you're not familiar with the finer points of backgammon, Handmark includes a thorough instruction manual that's accessible right in the game (tap Info | Instructions). If you want to take back a bad move, tap Game | Undo Move. Need a hint? Tap Game | Hint. Yes, Backgammon is pretty easy to operate. Our work here is done. Go forth and gammon.

Killer Tip *Moving your pieces in Backgammon can seem a little confusing at first. After you roll the dice, the one on the left represents your first move. If you want your first move to be the die on the right, tap either die to swap their positions. Now tap the piece you want to move.*

FIND IT ON THE CD
Backgammon, $14.99
Handmark
www.handmark.com

49 Billiard Master

Shoot Some Stick

You don't have to be a big fan of pool—or even billiards—to enjoy Billiard Master, a way-cool game that lets you play rounds of 8-ball and 9-ball against a human or computer opponent. Sure, your PDA's stylus makes for an awfully small cue stick, but at least you don't have to stand around a smoky bar waiting for a table (unless you enjoy that sort of thing).

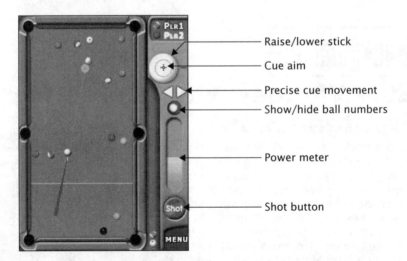

Raise/lower stick
Cue aim
Precise cue movement
Show/hide ball numbers
Power meter
Shot button

Billiard Master includes a practice mode so you can get a feel for the controls, which are generally quite easy. For your break, you can tap and drag the cue ball anywhere below the scratch line (or just leave it in the center). Now it's time to line up your shot. By default, Billiard Master's hint mode is on (visit the Options menu if you want to turn it off), meaning you see a line representing the exact trajectory of your ball based on the position of the cue stick. Tap and drag the stick to line up your shot.

Use the white left/right arrows to finesse the aim. You can also adjust where you strike the ball—just tap and drag the crosshairs inside the green circle, located above the aim arrows. You can even change the angle at which you strike the cue ball. Tap and drag the little line to the right of the white ball.

Finally, decide how hard you want to hit the ball. Tap anywhere inside the power meter (just above the Shot button), then drag up and down until it's set at the desired strength. Tap Shot and watch the balls dance! Needless to say, you'll probably want to spend some time practicing before you challenge the computer—or that surly looking guy with a tattoo—to a game.

Not familiar with the rules of 8-ball and/or 9-ball? Tap Billiard Master's Help option for instructions on both. Now you're ready to rack 'em up!

Killer Tip *Dragging the cue stick is fine for lining up the basic direction of your shot, but you'll notice you can't always position it precisely where you want. Thus, take full advantage of the aiming arrows, which make hairline adjustments to the shot angle. And there's no shame in leaving the hint line on. You have to make some concessions to the fact that this isn't a real table—you can't lean down to make sure you have the perfect angle.*

FIND IT ON THE CD
Billiard Master, $19.95
DigYs
www.digys.com

50 | Text Twist

A Game That Boggles the Mind

If you look at the letters GEVAAS and immediately see "savage," you're sure to enjoy Text Twist, an elegant variation on Boggle and one of Rick's all-time favorite games. The premise is simple: you're given six scrambled letters and two minutes in which to build as many words as possible. To score the maximum number of points and move on to the next level, you have to unscramble the six-letter word.

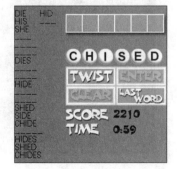

Text Twist has over 10,000 words in its dictionary, so you're not likely to run out anytime soon. If you get stuck while trying to build your words, you can tap the Twist button to reshuffle the letters. If you're really good, you'll get all the possible words before time runs out, and earn bonus points (and bragging rights) in the process.

Killer Tip *Astraware is responsible for some of the most popular PDA games on the planet. Ever heard of Bejeweled? The PDA version comes from Astraware. We also highly recommend BookWorm, Bounce Out, Insaniquarium, and especially Word Mojo, which is like Scrabble with a twist. You can download demos of these and other excellent Astraware games from the company's web site.*

FIND IT ON THE CD

Text Twist, $14.95
Astraware
www.astraware.com

51 PocketConquest

What's Life Without a Little Risk?

What family doesn't have fond memories of sitting around the Risk board, vying for global domination and ultimately getting into a huge fight? The only fight you can get into with PocketConquest is with your Pocket PC, but that doesn't make it any less satisfying. This Risk clone captures all the fun of the boardgame. Just try not to whip your PDA at a brick wall if you get frustrated by unfriendly dice.

At the outset, you and up to seven computer players (only one human can participate, alas) divvy up the world's countries, then place your troops as strategically as possible. While there's strength in numbers, there's also the random element that comes from "rolling the dice." If you have eight troops and you're attacking a country with three, you're likely to capture it—but there's always the possibility you'll lose. Let the insanity begin.

Killer Tip *Want to play PocketConquest on your PC? You can, only it's called Conquest for Windows. It sells for $20, just like the Pocket PC version, but you can buy the two together for $30. Visit the developer's web site for details.*

FIND IT ON THE CD
PocketConquest, $20
Sean O'Connor's Windows Games
www.windowsgames.co.uk

52 Chopper Alley

Indulge Your Inner Jan-Michael Vincent

Jan-Michael Vincent...star of the cheesy '80s action show *Airwolf*...remember? The souped-up helicopter? The feathered hair? Ernest Borgnine? Dave still has posters taped to the walls of his bedroom.

Anyway, Chopper Alley is a helicopter-combat simulation reminiscent of the PC classic *Comanche*. (See, Jan-Michael Vincent flew a helicopter in the show, and Chopper Alley is a helicopter sim—get it? Yeah, it was a bit of a stretch. Dave's idea. Bad Dave!) You get to pilot six different choppers in 25 different missions—and the graphics must be seen to be believed.

These grayscale screenshots don't do the game justice, but check 'em out anyway:

Helicopters aren't the easiest aircraft to control, whether you're in the cockpit of a real one or at the helm of a computer (or, natch, PDA) simulation. Fortunately, Chopper Alley makes it reasonably simple, relying on your Pocket PC's d-pad to move your 'copter left, right, forward, and back. To fire your selected weapon, press the d-pad. (If your PDA's d-pad doesn't have this "action button" capability, meaning you can't press it, you won't be able to play the game. D'oh!) Tap Help from the main menu to see a complete illustration of Chopper Alley's controls.

Killer Tip   *In the game's Options menu, you can adjust various graphics settings that make a big difference in how the game looks. For instance, we prefer the landscape screen orientation, which rotates the game 90 degrees for "widescreen" play. (When you do this, the d-pad controls change accordingly. What was previously left is now up, and so on.) And if your Pocket PC has a relatively fast processor, set the Draw Distance and Image Quality levels to Very High. (If these actions cause the game to slow down too much, you may have to drop them down again. Experiment until you find the ideal settings.)*

When you start the game, you'll need to select which helicopter you want to fly—each model has different attributes that can affect mission success—and your weapons loadout. The number of weapons you can carry depends on the number of pylons attached to the helicopter. This number ranges from two to eight—and there's one chopper that has no pylons at all. Instead, it carries passengers—useful for those search-and-rescue missions.

Once in flight, tap the bar at the right-hand side of the screen to adjust your altitude. You can also tap the Strafe control to move your aircraft left and right while still facing the same direction (unlike the standard left/right controls, which rotate the helicopter).

Happy carpet-bombing!

Killer Tip *At press time, Handango (www.handango.com) was offering a special bundle—Chopper Alley Classic Collection—for just $4.99. You're probably thinking it's a stripped-down version or something, but it actually comes with four more missions than the Zio version.*

FIND IT ON THE CD
Chopper Alley, $19
Zio Interactive
www.ziointeractive.com

53 Darxide EMP

Outer Space Adventures

As Chopper Alley proves, a Game Boy has nothing on your Pocket PC when it comes to action games. Of course, Chopper Alley is all about helicopters. If you prefer to blow things up in space rather than on the ground, don't miss Darxide EMP. It reminds us of the classic PC games Elite and X-Wing, shoehorned into a Pocket PC.

The game is a pretty straightforward arcade shooter. Blast everything in sight—asteroids, alien ships, and so on—while collecting weapons upgrades and energy crystals and rescuing stranded miners. Your Pocket PC's d-pad is used to control your ship—the voice-record button fires your selected weapon, though you can change any of the button settings in the game's Options menu.

Killer Tip *If you enjoy this kind of outer-space adventure, we also recommend Anthelion (www.pdamill.com), Interstellar Flames (www.xengames.com), and RocketElite (www.rocketelite.com). They're not only fun, they're ideal for making your non-PDA-carrying friends jealous.*

54 PDA Playground

Keep the Kids Entertained

As ideas go, PDA Playground can't be beat. It turns your handheld into a miniature game room, complete with six minigames and activities for kids aged 3–7. We've long been fans of this idea, as a PDA can be the perfect diversion for long car rides and other patience-draining situations. The software cleverly "locks out" all buttons and icons, so there's no way your kids can accidentally erase data or switch to another program. In fact, you can add other third-party programs to PDA Playground's kid-friendly interface, so the little ones aren't limited to the software's six modules.

Speaking of which, PDA Playground's games are a mixed bag—but in a good way. Draw provides a paintbrush, color palette, eraser, fill tool, and spray paint, all for use on blank "paper." Paint (see Figure 4-2) sports the same tools, but offers 26 coloring-book pages with things like cats and teddy bears. ScratchOff requires kids to scribble all over the screen, thereby revealing one of the aforementioned pictures.

FIGURE 4-2   No crayons required for Paint, one of PDA Playground's six kid games. It lets your little one play with a digital coloring book.

FollowMe is a nice Simon-like memory game that uses animals, while PuzzlePath is a clever take on those old arrange-the-tiles games, except that here there's an animated little person you have to guide around a path. Finally, there's Match, a Concentration-style memory game we didn't think much of at first, but Rick's daughter Sarah has fun with it.

Killer Tip *Don't forget that to get out of PDA Playground, or even to ActiveSync your PDA, you must first exit the program.*

FIND IT ON THE CD
PDA Playground, $19.95
DataViz
www.dataviz.com

Chapter

A Handier Pocket PC

Like your Pocket PC? After this chapter, you'll love your Pocket PC. Sure, your PDA comes with some cool applications and makes it easy—heck, fun—to manage your day. But in this chapter, we've rounded up a slew of cool applications that go beyond what you'll find in the box and give your PDA a whole new dimension. Have you ever wanted to jot notes on your Pocket PC's Today screen? Command your PDA via voice? Keep track of birthdays and anniversaries all in one handy screen? Make your PDA more secure without having to remember an arcane password? It's all in here.

55 | Time Recorder

Where Does the Time Go?

Maybe we're getting old, but time seems to fly by these days, and we have precious little to show for it. Sure, Dave has managed to collect the phone numbers for all nine celebrities on *Hollywood Squares,* and Rick has a really cool collection of knitting needles, but the fact remains that neither of us can really account for where the hours go each day.

That's why we consider Time Recorder a godsend—and if you need to track your time as well, you might too. Time Recorder is a simple program that makes it easy to track how you spend your day. It uses the concept of projects and tasks, making it easy to get a total time count for your day or just focus on specific tasks and projects. To use the program, simply enter tasks into the program's calendar, and then occasionally create a summary report to tell you how your time is being used.

Here's how to get started with Time Recorder:

1. When you start the program, you're initially in the Day view, which should be empty. Let's add a new task. Tap and drag the stylus in the vertical time bar to specify a task that runs through part of your morning.

2. You'll next be taken to a dialog box to create your task. You need to specify what project this task is part of, then specify the task, and finally adjust the date and time, if necessary. Since you don't already have a project created, tap the button to the right of the project list menu.

3. Tap Add, and create a project name and description. Be sure to set the color, which is how it will appear in the Day view. If you stick with black, which is the default, you won't be able to see the text. Tap OK to save this information, then tap Done to return to the original dialog box.

4. Select the project you just made and then tap the task creation button. Follow the same procedure to create a task—tap Add, enter a name and description, and so on.

5. When you've set up the task to your satisfaction, tap OK. You should see the task appear in the Day view:

From here, it's much easier to create tasks, since the project is already established. When you have loaded your Day view with tasks and you're ready to assess your time management, tap the Reports tab. Choose a date range, pick one or more projects to include in the report, and then tap the Generate button. You can display just the projects or break out the report into details with tasks:

```
Time Recorder          ◀€ 1:45  ok
From  1 /29/04    ▼  to  1 /29/04    ▼
Projects                        ▼  🗑
From : 1/29/04 To : 1/29/04              ▲
--------------------------------------
101 Book
   Editing
      editing chapters 1-3
                        01:45           ≡
      write ch 4|
                        03:00
--------------------------------------
--------------------------------------
TOTAL : 04:45  (hh:mm)                   ▼
Entries        ▼  │ Generate │  Export
Day View │ Project │ Summary │ Reports  ◀▶
Edit Tools Help  ⍰              ⌨  ▲
```

Killer Tip *You can tap the Export button to incorporate these reports in Word or Excel. It's a great way to show the boss how watering his plants every day is really limiting your ability to devote time to world peace.*

FIND IT ON THE CD
Time Recorder, $15
Owlseeker Solutions
www.owlseeker.com

56 Agenda Fusion

Supercharge the Calendar

Don't get us wrong. We like the personal information-management tools built into the Pocket PC. But we think you'll agree that they're not that well integrated. So if you're like us and tired of having to hop between Pocket Outlook's individual applets—Calendar, Contacts, Tasks, and so on—you owe it to yourself to try Agenda Fusion. And we do mean try: the company lets you take it for a 14-day spin, and we've included that version on the CD. If you like it, you'll probably find that $30 is a small price to pay for such an invaluable asset.

Agenda Fusion takes a two-pronged approach to information management. It groups the core apps into a single application, making them much easier to access and navigate, and then it pumps them full of new features. Better still, there's no real learning curve, as you're working in familiar areas.

One look at the program's many views—all of them accessible via a row of tabs across the bottom of the screen—and you'll be sold. There are a half-dozen calendar views, all available from the first menu. The Today view, an enhanced version of the Today screen that the Pocket PC comes with, lists the day's tasks and appointments. The difference here, however, is that the tasks are listed rather than grouped, so you can check them off without having to leave the screen. You can also create new items (tasks, contacts, appointments, etc.) immediately just by tapping an icon. We also like the Agenda view. It expands things a bit by listing a select number of days (five is the default) in an at-a-glance format. Other views, like the Week and Month views, look like more traditional calendar layouts, and they let you shuffle your appointments around with drag-and-drop simplicity.

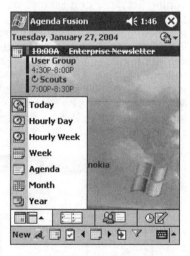

Agenda Fusion really shines with tasks and contacts. In the Task view, you can color-code your items and group them using a wide variety of criteria (category, date complete, priority, etc.). As for the contact list, its best feature is a preview pane that displays contact information while you browse. It doesn't sound too earth shattering, but it's a terrific improvement. One thing that is really cool: you can attach images of your contacts to their entries, letting you see pictures of people when you access their data on the Pocket PC.

While Pocket Outlook doesn't give you many tweaking options, Agenda Fusion lets you modify colors and font sizes for virtually every screen, so you get to decide how your data will look—and how much of it will fit onscreen.

With more features than we have space to list and an unbeatable umbrella interface for its superb information-management apps, Agenda Fusion deserves permanent residence on every Pocket PC handheld. Try it out!

FIND IT ON THE CD
Agenda Fusion, $29.95
DeveloperOne
www.developerone.com

57 ListPro

Turbocharge the To Do List

If you're like Dave, Rick, or Santa Claus, you like to make lists. Lists make the world go 'round. We make shopping lists, packing lists, to do lists, checklists, and reminders. And while the Tasks list that comes with your Pocket PC is good enough to get the job done a lot of the time, it's anemic, lacking Olympic-class features that folks like Santa need from their list-making software. So when we sat down to write this book, we made sure to find a better alternative to the Tasks program.

The alternative is ListPro, from Ilium Software. This is the program for folks who don't just make an occasional list, but who live and die by their to dos, checklists, notes, and reminders. When you tap the New menu to create a new list in ListPro, you are greeted by not just a generic list, but also a wide array of templates for all sorts of situations:

No matter which kind of list you choose, you can customize the fields and columns that your list contains. It can be a simple checklist, for instance, or a complex, database-like production in which you can track a half-dozen facts. You can record details about eBay auctions, for instance, track your DVD collection, or find the best products and prices when you go stereo shopping.

And your lists don't have to be "flat," either. If you are creating a complex list, you can indent items so that they appear to be subordinate to items above them. You can change indentation just by tapping and dragging items onscreen. That's not all. Your lists can include alarms, highlighting in a variety of colors, free-form text notes, and more. This is one of the most impressive list managers for the Pocket PC, and that's why you'll find it on the CD.

FIND IT ON THE CD

ListPro, $19.95
Ilium Software
www.iliumsoft.com

Hypercharge Your Notes

Few inventions in the twentieth century have had as much impact on office life as the ubiquitous sticky note. The desktop computer and electricity don't hold a candle to those yellow squares of paper that, in some cubicles, actually replace wallpaper.

And in a way, your Pocket PC's Notes program is a sort of portable sticky-note generator. It doesn't stick to the wall, but it's a great way to remind yourself about things you need to do or remember. Electric Pocket's BugMe! is a souped-up alternative to Notes that better mimics the best aspects of sticky notes. Not only do BugMe! notes accommodate text and graphics, but they do things that real yellow stickies only dream about—like automatically reminding you about their contents.

BugMe!, at its heart, is a sketching program. You can draw free-form shapes on the Pocket PC's screen by drawing directly on the screen with your stylus. You can also jot down short notes in "digital ink." To create a new note, you have two choices. You can tap the New menu at the bottom of the Today screen and choose a BugMe! note, or you can launch BugMe! and launch a new note from the Note menu. Then just use the drawing and text tools like you would any simple painting program.

All that is cool, but not extraordinary. BugMe! is unique in that it allows you to attach alarms to each of your notes. At a preset time, your BugMe! memo pops onto the screen, complete with a snooze button, and vies for your attention.

Here's how to set an alarm:

1. If you don't immediately see a blank screen, create a new note by choosing New | New Large from the menu.

2. Draw anything you like on the screen using the various pen tools at the top of the screen. You can adjust the pen thickness and style, as well as switch to an eraser to selectively undo your strokes.

3. There are two ways to add text to your note. You can draw using digital ink or tap the note button at the top left of the screen and enter any text you like.

4. When you're done, you can set an alarm to be reminded about the note. Tap the alarm box at the bottom of the screen and choose any sort of alarm you like. You can set it to go off in a certain number of minutes, hours, or days, or choose Custom, which opens an Alarm Details dialog box. Use it to set an alarm for any date and time you choose.

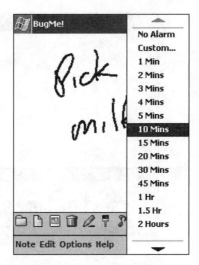

FIND IT ON THE CD
BugMe!, $19.95
Electric Pocket
www.electricpocket.com

59 Decuma OnSpot

Better Handwriting Recognition

Your Pocket PC comes with a few different ways to enter data—the onscreen keyboard, Transcriber, and Block Recognizer, to be precise. They all have their advantages, but Pocket PC fanatics are always looking for a better way to enter data. Specifically, they're looking for a better handwriting recognition system. There are quite a few alternatives out there, but we're pretty excited about a new one called Decuma OnSpot.

Decuma OnSpot is designed, according to the company that created it, to work more like pen and paper than existing handwriting schemes. And in a lot of ways, we agree. When you use Decuma OnSpot, you see a single entry area, like this:

To enter text, just print a letter at a time (don't connect your letters, like you would in script), and they are translated as you go. So far, so good—but much like many other systems you may have used. Here's where it gets different. If you see a mistake, just write the corrected letter right over the top of the wrong character. To delete a character, draw a backward dash over the letter. Want to insert a space between two letters? Draw a carat (an insertion symbol) over the top of the appropriate letter. It's a lot like writing on paper. And you make all your corrections in the Decuma OnSpot box before the text is ever placed into the open Pocket PC document.

Notice that there are two tabs atop the Decuma OnSpot writing space. By default, you enter text in the alphabetic region. To enter just text and symbols, tap the second tab. Remember—you can enter numbers in the alphabetic tab, but the numbers and symbols tab will not recognize any ordinary text.

![Notes screen showing "It was the best of times" with handwriting input panel]

When you are ready to insert your text into a document, you have two choices:

- Tap the right arrow at the right edge of the screen.
- Start writing a new word at the far left of the screen, to the left of the starting point of the existing text.

You can try Decuma OnSpot for free to see if you like it. If you're like us, you will prefer Decuma OnSpot to most of the handwriting alternatives available for the Pocket PC.

Killer Tip *You'll get the best results from Decuma OnSpot when you write perfectly straight, not at a slant. And remember not to connect letters—Decuma OnSpot does not handle script.*

FIND IT ON THE CD
Decuma OnSpot, $29.95
Decuma
www.decuma.com

60 Tapless

Faster Data Entry

When you consider all of the input alternatives available for the Pocket PC, you tend to get the impression that very few people like the built-in Block Recognizer, Transcriber, and virtual Keyboard utilities that are supposed to help you input data into your PDA. Indeed, we just got done telling you about Decuma OnSpot, and hot on its heels we have another option: a clever little program called Tapless.

Tapless is an incredibly flexible, powerful word completion–style text input system. The basic premise: you input a few characters, then browse for the complete word from a comprehensive dictionary stored on your Pocket PC. As you enter more characters, Tapless drills further into the dictionary, refining your options. And the program gets easier to use with time, since commonly used words are color coded for faster access.

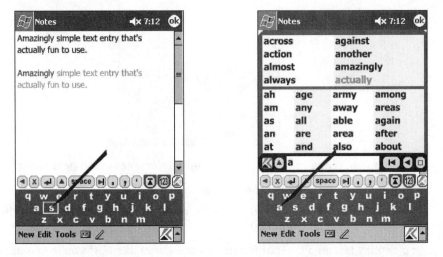

One of the best aspects of Tapless is that you can use the program in various ways. You can tap on a word to immediately insert it in your open document, or use gestures to add the word with punctuation. Swipe the stylus up across the word to capitalize it; swipe right to insert it with a space; swipe left to add a period. Or you can explore "word webs" that let you build complex words a prefix at a time. To get to dogsledding, for instance, tap and hold dog. Then pick dogs from the list, and finally find dogsledding. And the only character you had to type was a *d*. Of course, whether that process is actually faster than simply typing the word is debatable.

Tapless comes with a desktop configurator that lets you customize the interface; you can choose from among a few different keyboards—including QWERTY, Dvorak, and a Graffiti clone called Picasso. You can also tweak the size of the on-board dictionary, screen colors, and stylus tapping behavior. That said, using Tapless is almost like playing a game; you have to love the idea of throwing away the shackles of Block Recognizer and you have to enjoy hunting the screen in search of your next word. In our experience, Tapless can be a very fast, efficient way to enter data—but only if you like the rather unusual method of entering words. But what the heck? The trial version on the CD is free, so you may as well give it a spin.

FIND IT ON THE CD

Tapless, $29.95
Synaptek Software
www.tapless.com

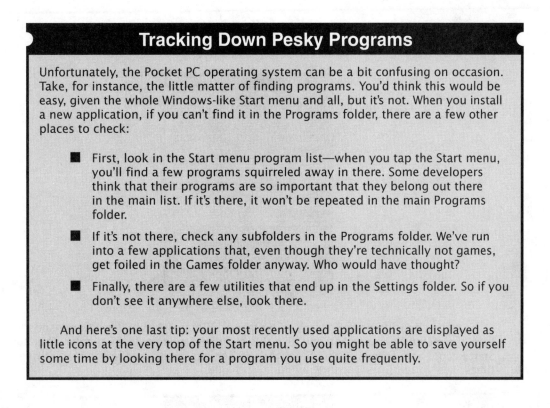

Tracking Down Pesky Programs

Unfortunately, the Pocket PC operating system can be a bit confusing on occasion. Take, for instance, the little matter of finding programs. You'd think this would be easy, given the whole Windows-like Start menu and all, but it's not. When you install a new application, if you can't find it in the Programs folder, there are a few other places to check:

- First, look in the Start menu program list—when you tap the Start menu, you'll find a few programs squirreled away in there. Some developers think that their programs are so important that they belong out there in the main list. If it's there, it won't be repeated in the main Programs folder.

- If it's not there, check any subfolders in the Programs folder. We've run into a few applications that, even though they're technically not games, get foiled in the Games folder anyway. Who would have thought?

- Finally, there are a few utilities that end up in the Settings folder. So if you don't see it anywhere else, look there.

And here's one last tip: your most recently used applications are displayed as little icons at the very top of the Start menu. So you might be able to save yourself some time by looking there for a program you use quite frequently.

61 | VoiceGo!

Control Your PPC by Voice

POWER APP

We'll admit it—we're hopeless sci-fi geeks. We love *Star Trek*, *Star Wars*, *Babylon 5*... even that new version of *Battlestar Galactica* that was on the Sci-Fi channel last year. And what is more sci-fi-ish than anything else? That's right...voice recognition! What could be cooler than that? (Excepting laser guns, transporter beams, and women dressed in shiny miniskirts?) That's right...nothing is cooler!

That's why we highly recommend that you try VoiceGo!, a surprisingly effective voice recognition program that lets you launch any program on your Pocket PC just by speaking a command.

To use VoiceGo!, you need to create some voice commands and assign them to programs on your Pocket PC. Start the program and you'll see a list of applications:

Start by choosing VoiceGo | Voice Commands | Create/Modify Voice Commands from the menu. Next, tap Add and give this command a name, like Calendar. Then tap Start Record and, following the directions you see onscreen, say the command three times.

With the voice command created, close the dialog box and return to the program list. Find the program that you want to associate with the command (in this case, the Calendar). Tap the application and then tap Assign Command. Choose the command from the list and tap the Select button.

![VoiceGo! application screen showing a list of applications with Name, Voice, and Path columns, with Run application, Assign command, and Unlink command buttons]

You're done! Now you can test the command by speaking it aloud; if it works, the application should start a few moments later.

Killer Tip *You can control whether VoiceGo! is listening for commands by visiting the VoiceGo | Voice Commands menu and choosing to turn listening on or off.*

FIND IT ON THE CD
VoiceGo!, $9.95
PDAWin
www.pdawin.com

62 | NotesToday

Notes at Home

So there you are—in your car, listening to a song on the radio. The announcer tells you its name—"I think I Love You," by the Partridge Family. You feverishly look for somewhere to write it down so you can run out and buy the record later in the week. But you don't have time to fumble with launching a program on your Pocket PC. You want to be able to turn on your PDA and start writing instantly. Is it possible? Can it be done? Sure it can.

NotesToday is a cool little note-taking program for your PDA that lives right where you need it most: on the Today screen, available the moment you turn on your Pocket PC. It's an idea so brilliant you wonder why it isn't built into the PDA to begin with.

After installing NotesToday, you'll see a new plug-in on the Pocket PC Today screen:

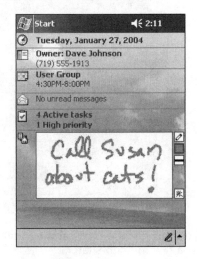

You can write a note using a variety of different pen thicknesses and colors, controlled from the buttons on the right side of the screen. There's also an erase button—the one at the bottom.

You can control other features, like the background color of the note. To do that, you need to access the NotesToday Options—tap the Home icon to the left of the note area and choose Options from the menu.

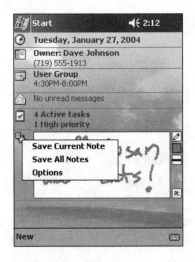

Here, in the options, you can see the settings for many of NotesToday's features. Keep in mind, though, that the note's size and total number of notes are only configurable in the registered version. In the trial version of the program, you're limited to a single note that's only 100 pixels high.

Height:	120	OK
Number of notes:	9	Cancel

Save path:

\Program Files\NotesToday

Background: Yellow

☐ Ask before clearing a note
☐ Collapsable   ☑ Note Border
☑ Auto Save

NotesToday Version 1.0.1

FIND IT ON THE CD

NotesToday, $5
enVision
evs.dellama.com

63 LoanTools

Everyday Loan Calculations

The financial world runs on a single question: what if? What if you bought a $20,000 car—what would the payments be? What if you want to retire with a million dollars—what would you have to do to save that much money? These are all classic financial planning questions, and unless you have a live-in financial planner, you might want to use a program like LoanTools to answer them.

The program is composed of five tabs that take you to screens for loans, savings, asset management, investments, and program options:

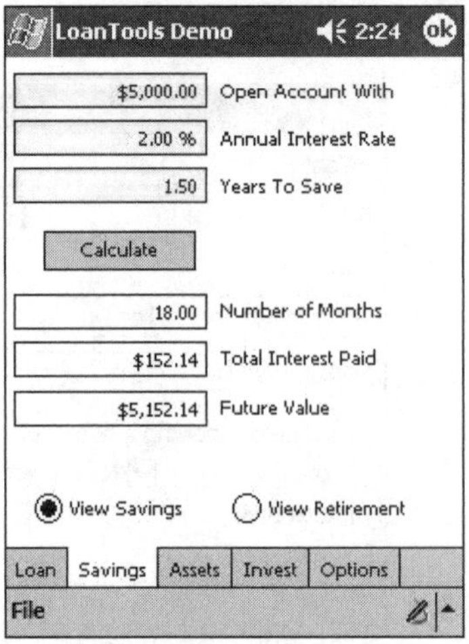

On each screen, it's easy to fill in the information you know to find the things you don't. On the Loan tab, for instance, you can find the monthly payments, number of payments, interest costs, and total payments for a loan by providing a few initial details like the loan amount, interest rate, and down payment. The program will even generate an amortization table for you.

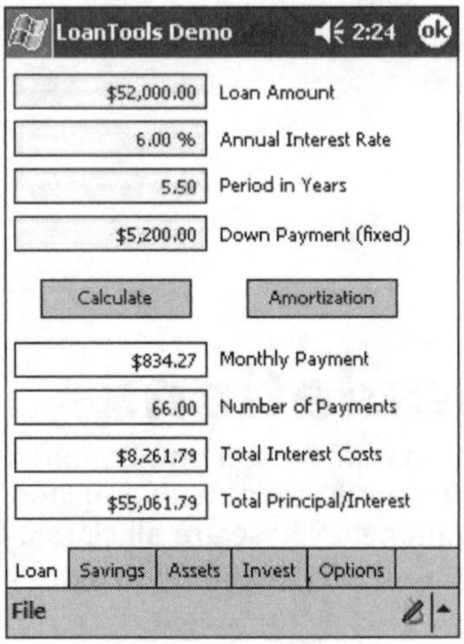

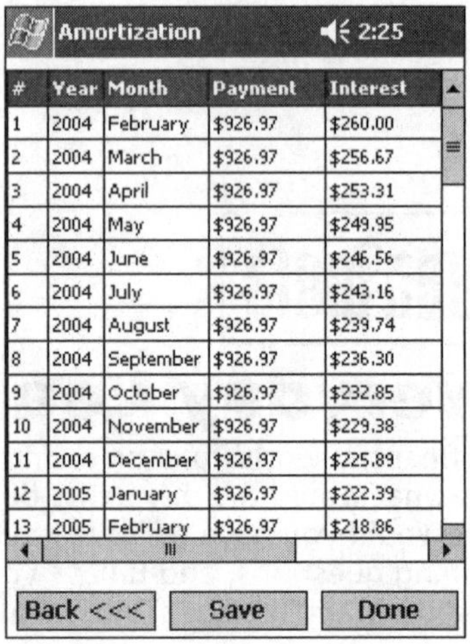

The PDA is a perfect instrument for taking a financial calculator everywhere you go. That way, you can run the numbers on that sweet-looking plasma-screen TV while you're in the store, before you surrender your credit card. Try out the demo on the CD.

FIND IT ON THE CD
LoanTools, $24.95
PPC Software
www.handango.com

64 Unit Converter

How Many Furlongs in a Liter?

Rick called Dave the other day. Rick, it turns out, is not very technically minded. Here's how the conversation went:

"Dave, how many furlongs are in a liter?"

Dave replied: "Well, Rick, a furlong is a measure of distance, while a liter is a measure of volume."

Silence.

"Rick?"

"Yes?"

"One is distance. The other is volume."

"So," Rick asked slowly, "how many of one is in the other?"

Dave paused. "Rick, it's like apples and oranges. How many apples are in an orange?"

Rick: "Three, I think."

After that call, Dave suggested that Rick install a copy of Unit Converter on his Pocket PC. Unit Converter is a very simple application that does exactly what the title claims: it lets you find the equivalency between various units. The program includes a large number of categories—stuff like length, area, mass, acceleration, temperature, volume, and more. In fact, the program includes categories for somewhat obscure units only commonly used by engineers—torque, viscosity, and power, for instance. To get started, just pick the appropriate category from the list:

Then choose the units you want to convert. In length, for instance, you might need to know how many miles are in 10 kilometers. Choose km at the

top and miles below. Then enter **10** in the km line, and you'll find that it's 6.2 miles. Now you know how far you ran on all those 10K races.

You can change the number on either line and it's automatically recalculated and converted on the other line.

This program is free, but there is a commercial version of Unit Converter that, for $5, adds a few extra features like custom units. Equipped with that, you might finally be able to tell Rick how many furlongs are in a liter.

FIND IT ON THE CD

Unit Converter, Free
Maximilian Wimmer
www.handango.com

65 DateMate

Remembering Important Dates

When Dave bought his first computer in 1987 (an Amiga 500, in case you're curious), his justification for buying it—to his brand-new wife, at least—was that he could use it to track birthdays and anniversaries.

"When we have a computer, we can automate all those important dates and never miss sending out a birthday card again!"

That worked okay, but not as well as Dave had hoped. After all, it took time and energy to look up birthdays on a desktop computer, and Dave is a fundamentally lazy person. But what if your PDA tracked all of those dates? If it's always in your pocket anyway, wouldn't that work better?

That's the idea behind DateMate. DateMate displays all of your upcoming birthdays and anniversaries in one place. No need to hunt through a calendar or search your contacts. It's all right there on one screen:

```
┌──────────────────────────────────┐
│ 🎴 DateMate        📢 2:27  ⊗   │
├──────────────────────────────────┤
│ All Categories              ▼    │
├──────────────┬──────────┬────────┤
│ Name         │ Date △   │   #    │
├──────────────┼──────────┼────────┤
│🎂Johnson Dave │  5/18/04 │   39   │
│🦅4th of July  │   7/4/04 │  227   │
│🎗Johnson Dave │  8/29/04 │   16   │
│🎗Broida Rick and S... │ 9/9/04 │ 8 │
│🎂Broida Rick and S... │10/13/04│ 1 │
│                                  │
│                                  │
│                                  │
├──────────────────────────────────┤
│ New Events Tools Help      ▦ ▲   │
└──────────────────────────────────┘
```

The best part about DateMate is that there are two ways to get entries into the program. You can tap the New menu and complete a form to enter the name, date, and type of event:

```
┌──────────────────────────────────┐
│ 🎴 DateMate        📢 2:28  ok   │
├──────────────────────────────────┤
│ Last Name:  [              ]     │
│                                  │
│ First Name: [              ]     │
│                                  │
│ Category:   [No Category   ▼]    │
│                                  │
│ Date:        1 /27/04      ▼     │
│                                  │
│ ☐ Repeating (Yearly)            │
│                                  │
│ Reminder:   [None      ▼]       │
│                                  │
│ at 8:00 AM  [1  ▼][day(s)  ▼]   │
│              before event        │
│                                  │
│   [   OK   ]  [  Cancel  ]       │
│                                  │
├──────────────────────────────────┤
│ Edit                       ▦ ▲   │
└──────────────────────────────────┘
```

Or, a somewhat easier process is to simply import the events from Contacts. If you have already entered birthdays and anniversaries, this is a snap. Choose Events | Import

Events from Contacts and, after a few moments, you'll fill the program with all the dates you could ever hope to write greeting cards for.

DateMate doesn't limit you to birthdays and anniversaries. When you create a new event, the Category list includes entries for holidays, business events, parties, vacations, and more.

Killer Tip *You can sort your DateMate events in a variety of ways, but we find that sorting by date is best— you see the next birthday or anniversary right at the top of the list. To sort by date, just tap the Date header at the top of the screen.*

FIND IT ON THE CD
DateMate, $9.95
MobiMate
www.mobimate.com

66 visual Key

Stop! Who Goes There?

We hate passwords. We hate memorizing passwords. We hate typing passwords. In fact, there's only one thing we like about passwords: they tend to keep our data safe.

And therein lies the problem. You can teach your Pocket PC to use a password, but actually using it is so annoying that you no doubt stop after a short time, exposing all the precious data on your PDA to theft if your device is ever lost or stolen. There has to be a better way.

Indeed there is. If you have a Pocket PC with a biometric scanner, then your fingerprint is all you need to get into your device. That's pretty easy. But if you don't have one of those super-fancy PDAs, then visual Key is your next best bet.

The idea behind visual Key is this: instead of entering an easy-to-forget string of letters and numbers into your PDA every time you want to use it, why not get in visually—by tapping in a secret location on a digital image? You can set up a sequence of taps as simple or as complicated as you like. We've tried visual Key with just one tap—right on someone's eyeball, for instance—and we've configured visual Key to wait for four or five taps. You have to hit the right locations in the right order for the program to let you in.

When you first install the program, you'll need to set up a password. Here's how:

1. Start the program and click Cancel when it asks for a registration number. You can test it for 30 days without one.

2. You should see a step-by-step wizard for setting up your password. Tap Step 1: Options/Bitmap.

3. Tap the Select Picture button and find an image on your Pocket PC that you want to use. It should be about 320×240 pixels in size, so you may need to adjust it on the PC first.

4. Assign a password in the Hotsync Password box atop the screen. This is what you will need to enter in your PC to perform an ActiveSync.

5. Tap the Save button.

6. Now tap Step 2: Define Your New Password. Make several taps on the image in places you will easily remember, such as in the image below. Also, keep track of the order in which you do these taps. When you're done, tap OK.

7. Tap Step 3: Verify and Save Your Password. Now reenter the taps and tap Verify. If it works, save the password.

Now, whenever you turn on your Pocket PC, you'll see this image. Tap in the right places and you'll get entry to your device. Of course, it's highly unlikely that anyone else will be able to figure out your code.

FIND IT ON THE CD
visual Key, $15
sfr GmbH
www.viskey.com

Chapter 6

Learn Something

n case we haven't sufficiently driven home this point yet, your PDA is much more than just a pocket organizer—it's a pocket computer. And anything that smart riding around in your pocket should be able to teach you a thing or two. New vocabulary words, facts about France, dangerous drug interactions—that kind of thing. In this chapter, we look at software for students, teachers, and learners alike, as well as an indispensable tool for doctors and patients (hint: it has something to do with dangerous drug interactions).

67 Oxford American Desk Dictionary and Thesaurus

Festoon Your Vocabulary

For writers, students, and anyone else who relies on the written word, the two most indispensable books on the planet are a dictionary and thesaurus. Unfortunately, they're also two of the heaviest—which is why we love packing them into a PDA. Handmark's Oxford American Desk Dictionary and Thesaurus (let's call it ADD for short) contains over 150,000 entries. There's even a Word of the Day feature.

To look up any word, you simply start writing it in the search field. As you enter letters, a pick list begins to narrow in on your desired word. Thus, to look up, say, haberdasher, you need enter only "ha" before the word appears in the list. When you tap a word, ADD displays its pronunciation, part of speech, definition(s), and, where applicable, synonyms. The latter are hot-linked, meaning you can tap any one to see its definition. A "back" button would be welcome here, but at least ADD does have a pop-up list containing recently viewed words.

Ideally, ADD would give you the option of hearing each word pronounced, but that would likely require more storage space than most PDA users care to sacrifice. Speaking of which, the software requires a whopping 5.5MB of memory, so you may want to install it right to a memory card.

Killer Tip *If you have money to spare but not memory, you can buy ADD already loaded on a memory card. This version, also available from Handmark, sells for $49.99—$20 more than the software-only version. Just pop it in your PDA's card slot and the program loads automatically. It's a convenient solution, but we think you'd be better off buying the software and a third-party memory card, which you can do for about the same $50. That way you'll have room to store ADD and plenty of other programs.*

ADD puts a fast, attractive, easy-to-use dictionary and thesaurus in your pocket. Linguists amateur and professional, rejoice!

FIND IT ON THE CD
Oxford American Desk Dictionary and Thesaurus, $29.99 (MMC version, $49.99)
Handmark
www.handmark.com

68 emAnalogy

A PDA Is to a Duck as a Spoon Is To...

Although Rick wears his English-major badge with great honor, there was one area of the SATs that caused him to break out in cold sweats. See if it has the same effect on you:

Jute : Cotton, Wool :

A. Teryline

B. Silk

C. Rayon

D. Nylon

Oh, the humanity! Well, they say practice makes perfect, so if you're studying for a big test that's going to include these kinds of analogies (or you're just masochistic), stock your Pocket PC with emAnalogy for Pocket PC 2002. It comes with over 100 questions like the previous example, all designed to improve your language skills.

```
┌─────────────────────────────────────┐
│ I :Sword :: Thread :II               │
│                                      │
│  Ⓐ Dagger        Ⓟ Needle           │
│                                      │
│  Ⓑ Knife         Ⓠ Tailor           │
│                                      │
│  Ⓒ Warroir       Ⓡ Rope             │
│                                      │
│  Ⓓ Kill          Ⓢ Stitch           │
│                                      │
│  ❶ BR   ❷ DS   ❸ AP   ❹ CQ          │
│                                      │
│    Time : 11          Score : 0      │
│                                      │
│         [ Skip ]  [ Quit ]           │
└─────────────────────────────────────┘
```

You're given 20 seconds to answer each question, which makes emAnalogy feel more like a game (a brutal one, admittedly) than a study aid. If you're really adept, you can try its Double Analogy mode, in which you have to solve two analogies in the same 20 seconds.

If you've got another $12.95 to spare and a hankering for more wordplay, try emAnalogy II. It takes a slightly different approach, giving you three related words and challenging you to choose a like grouping of related words. Here's an example:

Smile : Laugh : Cry

A. Sit : Sleep : Play

B. Frown : Anger : Temper

C. Morning : Night : Day

D. Touch : Catch : Release

Are we having fun yet?

FIND IT ON THE CD
emAnalogy, $15.95
Encom Emsys Technologies
www.allmobileworld.com

4.0Student

Keep Track of School Assignments

For students in high school or college, organization is half the battle. There's so much information to keep track of—assignments, test dates, instructor info, class locations, grades, and so on—that it can interfere with a successful academic career. Enter 4.0Student, which stores all that information and more for fast and easy reference. It can even add coursework reminders to your appointment calendar and to do list.

4.0Student can seem a little intimidating at first, if only because you start with an almost entirely blank screen. Here's the step-by-step procedure for getting started:

1. Tap Class | New, then enter all the pertinent details regarding your class (name, course number, days and time, a web page if applicable, and so on). Tap OK when you're done.

2. If you want to add information about the instructor, tap the apple icon at the bottom of the screen, then record items like office hours, phone number, and e-mail address.

3. Add your first assignment, test, or other kind of coursework by tapping Class | Add Coursework. Here you can enter the due date, the corresponding textbook (only one, unfortunately), and your final score once the item has been graded. Notice, too, the options to add the coursework to your PDA's datebook or to do list. Just tap the corresponding button once you've filled in the name and due date, and 4.0Student will copy the data to the proper program.

4. If your instructor or school has a specific grading policy, tap Class | Grading Policy to adjust percentages and how they translate to letter grades.

Entering all this information on your PDA can be awkward and time-consuming. 4.0Student doesn't come with a desktop component for synchronization, but there is another option. It's called Fourostudent.net (see Figure 6-1), a Web-based service where you can type in all your class and coursework on your PC, then synchronize it with 4.0Student on your PDA. The service also enables you to print copies of your records and even share them online with teachers and other students. A one-year subscription to Fourostudent.net is included in the price of 4.0Student; a two-year subscription costs $10 more.

Killer Tip *Not sure if you can pull up your GPA by the end of the year? Use 4.0Student's What If feature to calculate how remaining tests and assignments will affect your final grade. Tap Tools | What If, and then plug in the grades you expect to get. Before you can do this, however, you have to enter all the upcoming coursework in 4.0Student's main screen.*

FIND IT ON THE CD

4.0Student, $29.99 (includes one year of Fourostudent.net)
Handmark
www.handmark.com

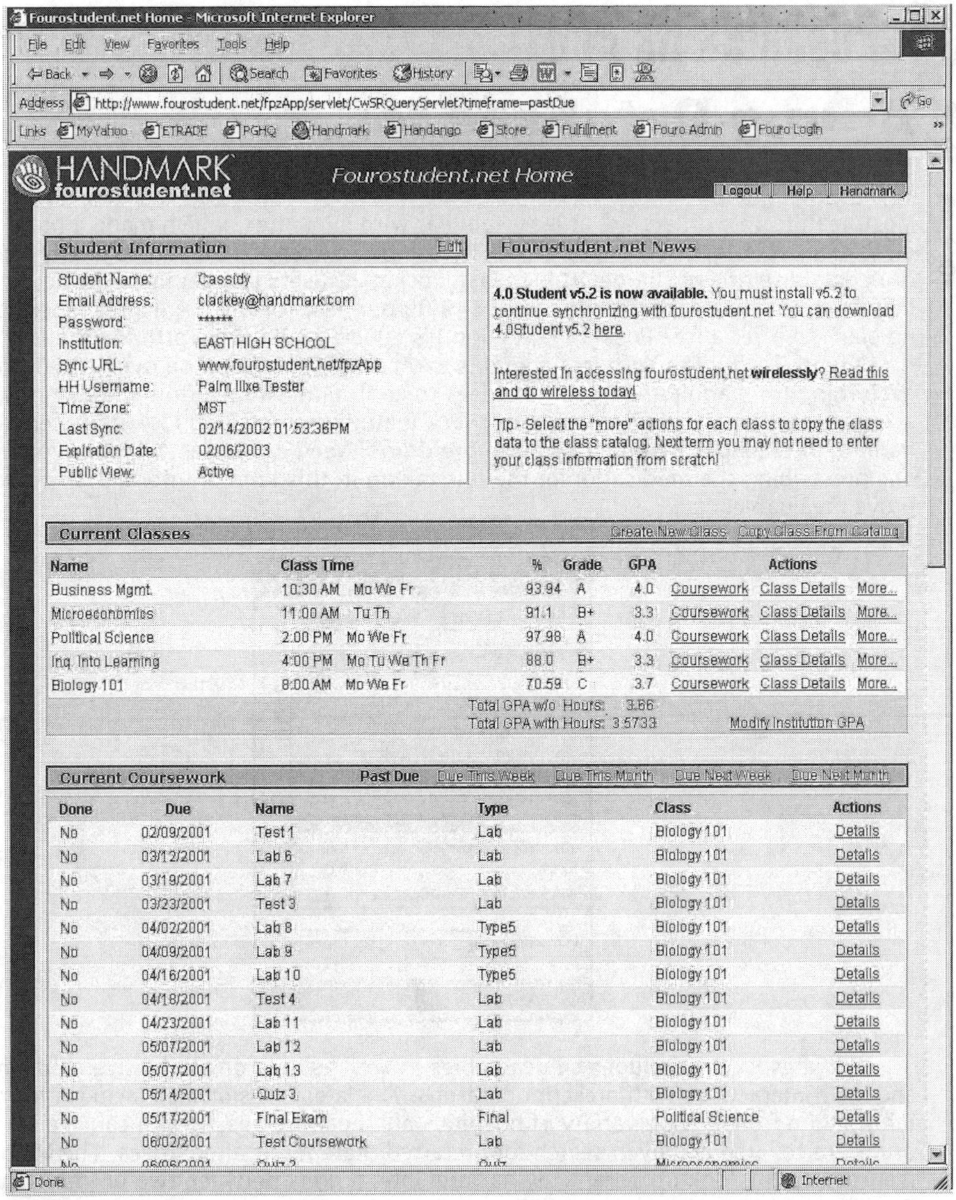

FIGURE 6-1   With Fourostudent.net, you can synchronize your 4.0Student data with the Web—and enter new data much more easily.

70 ePocrates Rx Pro

A Drug Database for Doctors and Patients

POWER APP

Most healthcare workers are at least familiar with ePocrates, which made a huge splash on the Palm platform a few years back by offering a comprehensive, regularly updated drug database free of charge. At long last, Pocket PC users can get in on the act, though they have to pay a subscription fee of $49.99 per year for the privilege. (ePocrates has no plans to offer a free Pocket PC version.) Is ePocrates Rx Pro worth the money?

Unequivocally. The software contains extensive information on over 2,800 drugs—everything from adult and pediatric doses to contraindications, drug interactions, and adverse reactions. There's also a Multicheck feature that lets you look up potentially harmful interactions between two or more drugs. Needless to say, whether you're the one prescribing the medication or the one taking it, this kind of information could prove invaluable.

ePocrates Rx Pro includes clinical tables as well as data on alternative medicines and their interactions with prescription drugs. The latest version also includes formulary information from a wide variety of hospitals and health plans, so you can see which drugs are covered and even search for preferred therapeutic alternatives. The Multicheck feature lets you look up potentially harmful interactions between two or more drugs. Finally, there's DocAlerts, which delivers clinical news from the FDA, CIC, and other organizations (some of them commercial in nature).

The software is easy to navigate thanks to the four tabs used to divide the main sections. Updates are downloaded to your Pocket PC via your computer's Internet connection, as with programs like AvantGo (see Chapter 9) and Vindigo (see Chapter 2). Thus, if you use America Online or some other dial-up service, make sure you're signed on before you connect your Pocket PC.

Killer Tip *Synchronizing with the ePocrates servers can add a couple extra minutes to the ActiveSync process. If you synchronize several times per day, you probably don't want to wait it out every time. Fortunately, you can set ePocrates Rx Pro to update just once per day—or even once per week. On your PC, click Start | Programs | ePocrates for Pocket PC | AutoUpdate Settings, then choose Update Data Daily (or Weekly, if you prefer).*

We think ePocrates Rx Pro is a bargain at twice the price, and a must-have resource for members of the healthcare community. However, because the software requires a subscription to the ePocrates service, we couldn't include it on the CD. There is, however, a link to the company's web site, where you can download the program.

FIND IT ON THE CD
ePocrates Rx Pro, Free
ePocrates, Inc.
www.epocrates.com

71 The 2004 World Almanac, Handheld Edition Bundle

A Knack for Almanacs

If ever a program made a case for converting printed reference works into electronic books, it's Town Compass's The 2004 World Almanac. Forget for a moment the obvious advantage: one less heavy, bulky book to carry around. The real benefit here is the speed with which you can find what you're looking for. All it takes is two or three taps to drill your way into the almanac's thousands of entries and focus on any single bit of data. Contrast that with a paper version, which requires you to skim through a table of contents or index, then flip pages and scan listings until you find the right entry. How nineteenth century!

Killer Tip *After you install the program, you might expect to find an icon called Almanac, World Almanac, or something like that. Instead, the icon you're after is DataViewer, which is the name of the program used to access the almanac database files. Why? Town Compass offers a variety of other reference titles as well, including encyclopedias, dictionaries, and even a bartender's guide. DataViewer is the program required to view all Town Compass e-books.*

The 2004 World Almanac consists of 16 different sections, each a separate database file that must be installed on your PDA (along with the DataViewer program). You don't have to install them all—you can pick and choose the ones you want. Just extract all the files contained in the Zip file, then run _Setup.exe. Now remove the check marks from any modules you don't want installed.

Town Compass Installer

Please select which components you
would like to install:

- ☑ Town Compass DataViewer applicati...
- ☑ Town Compass Arts - Media '03-D
- ☑ Town Compass Awards-Prizes '03-D
- ☑ Town Compass College Sports '03-D
- ☑ Town Compass Consumer Info '03-D
- ☑ Town Compass Olympics_Misc '03D
- ☑ Town Compass Personalities '03-D

[Install]
[Cancel]
[About...]

For the record, the databases range in size from about 350KB to 1.2MB, so installing them to a memory card is all but mandatory—especially if you plan to install them all.

Once you have all the necessary files installed on your PDA, tap DataViewer to start the program, and then tap the logo screen that appears. Now you'll want to choose which database to view, done by tapping the arrow at the top of the screen and selecting it from the list. Next, select a subject area from the main window, then a specific entry from the pop-up menu that appears. Tap Home at any time to return to the main screen.

FIND IT ON THE CD

The 2004 World Almanac, Handheld Edition Bundle, $11.95
Town Compass
www.pocketdirectory.com

72 FlashCards 101

Holy Education, Batman! It's the Flash Card!

When it comes to learning aids, nothing beats flash cards. Sure, memorization isn't really learning, but when you have a test to pass...well, do you want a good grade or do you want to argue education semantics? FlashCards 101 is an elegant tool for creating and studying card sets.

FlashCards consists of two programs: one for the Pocket PC, the other for Windows. That means that after expanding the Zip file, you need to run two different Setup.exe programs, one at a time (the order doesn't matter). From there, you use the Windows component to create your flash cards, then export them to your Pocket PC for on-the-go studying. (Unfortunately, you can't create cards right on your Pocket PC—you have to use the Windows applet.)

To build a card set, just type a question and answer in the appropriate fields, then click Confirm Card. FlashCards 101 also lets you add small image files to the Question and Answer fields, meaning you can study illustrations, pictures, and so on. The images themselves must be square if they're to appear properly, and you have to copy them to a specific folder on your hard drive: C:\Program Files\myPocket technologies\Images.

Killer Tip *Need a way to resize your images so they're more FlashCards-friendly? Most popular image-editing programs, such as Jasc Paint Shop Pro, make it easy to modify image sizes. However, if you don't own such a program and don't want to invest upwards of $100 or more, check out IrfanView (www.irfanview.com). This great little program requires very little hard drive space and enables you to view, resize, crop, and otherwise modify your images, then save them in your format of choice (FlashCards supports BMP, GIF, and JPG files). Best of all, IrfanView is free!*

FIND IT ON THE CD
FlashCards 101, $10.99
MyPocket Technologies
www.mypocket-technologies.com

73 Zaz Kids Alphabet

Teach the Tots

Rick, who has a pair of young children, loves the idea of using his PDA to teach and entertain them. It's perfect when there's unexpected time to kill, like waiting for your food in a restaurant or stuck in line at the post office. Instead of watching the kids go berserk from boredom, you can just pull out your PDA and have some fun.

Take Zaz Kids Alphabet. It's like an illustrated children's book, one that aims to teach kids the alphabet using flash card–like screens. Each of its 26 pages contains a colorful picture of an item and its corresponding letter. You flip pages by tapping the green onscreen arrows.

If you like that, you'll also want to check out Zaz Kids Numbers:

Zaz Kids Colors:

and Zaz Kids Shapes:

Needless to say, these are aimed at the toddler set. If your kids are a bit older, try the developer's Addition, Subtraction, Multiplication, and Division games.

Killer Tip *Want to read your little one a story? Palm Digital Media (www.palmdigitalmedia.com), seller of PDA-formatted e-books (see Chapter 3), offers a selection of illustrated children's books—perfect for when you need to keep your kiddo occupied for a few minutes. Titles include* The Berenstein Bears, My First Real Mother Goose, *and* Puddle's ABC.

FIND IT ON THE CD
Zaz Kids Alphabet (and other titles), $1.99 each
Zaz
www.handango.com

Improve Your PDA's Battery Life

As PDA's gain more features—fast processors, high-resolution color screens, music and video players—battery life suffers. First-generation handhelds could last for weeks on a pair of AAA batteries, but modern models can peter out after just a few hours of heavy use. Fortunately, there's an easy way to extend battery life: lower screen brightness.

We know, we know, you paid big bucks for that dazzlingly bright screen, and you'll be damned if you're going to dim it. Well, which would you rather have: a dim screen or a blank one? In all seriousness, by lowering the brightness level to 50 percent—or, better yet, 25 percent—you can keep your PDA running significantly longer. Obviously, this isn't necessary if you spend most of your time near your charging cradle, but for long trips, it's a worthwhile sacrifice. In fact, we'll bet that after a few minutes, you'll hardly even notice the screen being dimmer.

Chapter 7

Connected Tricks

The world it is a changin'. A few years ago, when PDAs were the hot new thing, it was enough to be able to check your schedule from an electronic organizer kept tucked in your pocket. These days, "connected" organizers—PDAs that have Wi-Fi, Bluetooth, or a cell phone built in—are the new thing, and everyone, it seems, wants one. Such a gadget can retrieve e-mail, let you surf the Web, and perhaps even make phone calls. The possibilities are staggering.

There are all kinds of ways to get your Pocket PC online. You can connect it to a cell phone with a connection cable and let the phone act like a modem. If you're a bit more adventurous, you can connect your phone and PDA wirelessly with infrared or Bluetooth. Of course, one of the most exciting trends in PDAs is the smartphone—models like the T-Mobile Pocket PC Phone Edition and the Motorola MPx200 Microsoft Smartphone are a combination of PDA and mobile phone that does pretty much everything in one smart little box. With wireless happening around us, we wrote this chapter to help you figure out how you can use your Pocket PC to join the fast-growing world of the Internet. (For a brochure on how *you* can make money on the Internet, send $5 cash or your credit card to Dave or Rick. Allow six weeks for delivery.)

Killer Tip *Even if you don't have a wireless Pocket PC, there are one or two apps in this chapter you can use. We'll point them out with a clever little tip like this one that you're reading right now.*

74 AvantGo

The Web—Without a Connection

POWER APP

Here's one sad truth to start the chapter. Until Pocket PCs get a bit larger, the Web simply won't fit in your pocket. Those two-inch screens are just too claustrophobic. Enter AvantGo, a free service that not only delivers Web-based content to your PDA, but also formats it to look pretty and readable. With every ActiveSync, AvantGo downloads your preselected channels—everything from news and stock reports to driving directions and movie show times—using your computer's Internet connection to ferry the data. Pretty slick—and did we mention it's free? You get 2MB of content—that can be as many as a dozen channels, depending upon how much data is included in each. Want more? You can upgrade to 8MB of AvantGo service for $20/year.

If your Pocket PC doesn't already have AvantGo installed, you can get it from this book's CD or by visiting the AvantGo web site. You'll need to set up an AvantGo account, complete with username and password.

To set up the channels you want to transfer to your PDA, go to the AvantGo web site and log in. The AvantGo site should look something like Figure 7-1; your currently selected channels appear on the right in a tab called My Device. You can browse the AvantGo web site and click any channel you like to add it to your personal AvantGo hot list.

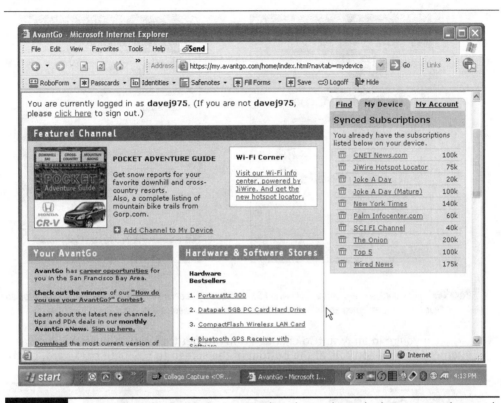

FIGURE 7-1 AvantGo's web site is where you subscribe to channels that you can then read on your PDA, even when you're not connected to the Internet.

Most AvantGo channels are configured to work well on a handheld device with limited memory. Sometimes you might want to customize the way channel content is delivered to your Pocket PC, though. Take *The Onion*, for instance. Dave loves to read this news parody web site each week while eating lunch, but the site is so large that many of the stories often aren't downloaded to the Pocket PC in their entirety. The solution? Dave increased the Maximum Channel Size from the default of 100KB to 500KB so it all fits on his PDA. To edit your channels as cleverly as Dave, open the AvantGo web page, log in, and click on a channel in the My Device tab. You should see the Channel Properties. Make your changes and click the Save Channel Changes button.

Ready to read some news on your Pocket PC while you eat lunch? On the Pocket PC, there's no actual AvantGo application—the channels show up in Internet Explorer. Start Internet Explorer and tap the AvantGo link at the bottom of the screen. After a moment, you'll see your channels. Just tap on one to start reading.

Note *If you don't see any channels in AvantGo, it's probably because you haven't installed the desktop software or successfully performed an ActiveSync with your channels selected yet.*

Once you're in an AvantGo channel, don't forget that you can use the standard Internet Explorer controls at the bottom of the screen to navigate backward, go to the Home page, and more.

FIND IT ON THE CD

AvantGo, Free
AvantGo
www.avantgo.com

75 VeriChat

Have a Chat

One of the most unexpected hits of the Internet age has certainly been instant messaging. Like e-mail, only instantaneous, IM allows people to converse in real time within text windows on their PC. That's great, but it begs the question: if your Pocket PC has the ability to connect to the Internet, can you take your IM sessions on the road with you? Absolutely! PDAapps offers VeriChat, a unified IM client for wireless Pocket PC devices. It connects you with all four key IM services: MSN Instant Messenger, Yahoo Instant Messenger, AOL Instant Messenger, and ICQ. Best of all, it delivers most of the common desktop IM features that you would expect from your PC right on the small screen.

You can choose to log in to all four services or any individual service when you sign into VeriChat. You see all of your desktop-configured chat buddies, separated into online and offline windows, and you can even set your availability for each service from icons at the top of the screen.

VeriChat supports multiple sessions that are persistent even if you log off and return to the program later. It's easy to switch between active chat sessions and even return to the main screen to open new ones.

Setting up the program is easy: you'll have no trouble completing the username and password for any of the services you subscribe to, and you can specify whether to log on automatically:

76 VITO VoiceDialer and VITO VoiceDialer PE

Dial Your Phone by Voice

We can't wait for the future.

"Phone, I need you to call Rick and let him know that since he lost another bet, he needs to pick up my laundry."

"Yes, Dave. I will also let him know that he is a 'loser,' as you put it, as per your standard instructions."

"Great. And car, drive me to Halle Berry's house. We have a date tonight."

"Certainly, Dave. Would you like me to stop by the florist to pick up her favorite flowers again?"

"No, I already asked the food processor to do that—it didn't have anything else to do today."

Yes, it's very implausible science fiction. After all, who would really believe that Halle Berry would date Dave? But while our appliances can't yet talk back to us, it's already quite possible to give our favorite gadgets commands by voice. Want to dial your phone by voice? Not a problem—many mobile phones have voice dialing built in. And thanks to VITO VoiceDialer, your Pocket PC can be dialed by voice as well.

Of course, this application isn't for everyone. You'll want to try out this program if your Pocket PC has some sort of connection to your mobile phone, such as Bluetooth. It's also perfect for Pocket PC Phone Edition devices that have both PDA and phone capabilities all in one. Notice, though, that there are two versions of VoiceDialer—the standard VoiceDialer app is for ordinary Pocket PCs. VoiceDialer PE is for Phone Edition devices.

After you install VITO VoiceDialer, your first stop should be the System tab in Settings. Here you need to configure VoiceDialer to do its magic—if you try to simply run the VoiceDialer application in the Programs folder, you'll get an error.

Start by telling the program how to connect to your mobile phone. Here, for instance, you can see it set up for a Bluetooth connection:

```
 Property            4:47  ok
Connection settings
 BTC1:  Bluetooth Port 1:        ▼

 Baud rate:           9600       ▼

 Data bits:           8          ▼

 Stop bits:           1          ▼

 Flow control:        none       ▼


 ☐ Don't Use HANG UP
 ☐ Use BT headset for Ericsson phones only
 [  Default  ]

Connection │ Learning │ About
```

Next, tap the Learning tab. This is the screen where you actually teach the program your voice commands. Pick an entry from the Contacts menu at the top of the screen. Choose which phone number associated with that contact that you want to dial, and tap the Record button. When you see the fuel gauge start to move across the screen, say the contact's name.

```
 Property            4:48  ok
Contacts
 American Airlines               ▼

 (800) 433-7300 Business         ▼

 [  Record  ] ████████
Learned commands: 2

 Advantage Rent A Car (800) 777-5500 B
 Airborne Express (800) 247-2676 B




 [ Play ] [ Delete ] [ Delete All ] [ Test ]

Connection │ Learning │ About
```

After you create a few entries, it's time to try dialing. Close the Settings application and run VoiceDialer from the Programs folder in the Start menu. When the program starts listening, say the name of the contact you want to dial. If it interprets you correctly, wait a moment and the number will dial automatically.

Voice Dialer ◀€ 4:48 ✖	Voice Dialer ◀€ 4:49 ✖
Recognition Process	**Recognition Process**
...listening to you...	...recognized as:
	Airborne Express
	(800) 247-2676 Business
	Recognition accuracy: 83 %
	[Correct] [Wrong]

Killer Tip *You don't have to tap the Correct button to get the phone to dial; it will happen automatically. You only need to intervene by tapping Wrong to abort an incorrectly interpreted phone number.*

FIND IT ON THE CD
VITO VoiceDialer and VITO VoiceDialer PE, $15.95
VITO Technology
www.vitotechnology.com

77 ThunderHawk
Surf the Web, Better

Why would anyone possibly want a new browser for their Pocket PC, especially one that costs about $50 per year, when they have Internet Explorer already installed for free?

Simple: the "Pocket" version of Internet Explorer is (let's be honest here) terrible. Just terrible. It does not have a landscape display mode, which means that you have to do a huge amount of scrolling to read web pages. Because the screen is so small, you can't see but a tiny portion of any web page at once. The program has no special help for entering URLs, which is troublesome on a small handheld device.

That's why we love ThunderHawk. Sure, it's a bit expensive, since it's subscription-based instead of a single charge, but you can use the demo on the CD to try it for a month and see if it is worth that much money to you.

ThunderHawk is a browser designed expressly for the Pocket PC. So it not only displays in landscape mode, but web pages are specially reformatted with optimized fonts to fit on the screen and be highly legible at the same time:

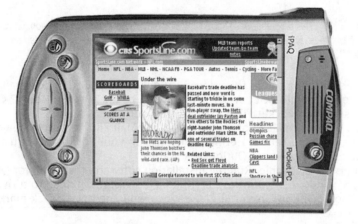

Getting around in ThunderHawk is a bit different than what you're already used to, but Bitstream does it this way to make best use of the Pocket PC's screen size and controls. There's no URL entry box or navigation controls onscreen, for instance. Instead, the program relies on the buttons on the front of your Pocket PC to do those things. Press button 1 or 2 to call up a URL entry system, complete with onscreen keyboard. As for page forward and page back, you control these functions with the other two buttons on the Pocket PC.

Give ThunderHawk a shot—you'll quickly find that reading pages and navigating around are far easier with this superior browser.

FIND IT ON THE CD

ThunderHawk, $49.95 per year
Bitstream
www.bitstream.com

78 OneMail

You've Got Mail! All of It!

A lot of folks enjoy taking their mail on the go. Instead of being a slave to their PC, these folks can sync their Pocket PC and read messages on the go—even if they don't have a wireless device. That's because you can synchronize your Pocket PC with Outlook's inbox every time you ActiveSync. You can reply, delete, and forward your messages from your Pocket PC, then all those changes will take place the next time you return to your office and put the Pocket PC back in its cradle. Sweet.

Killer Tip *This program doesn't need any kind of wireless Internet connection, so you can use it even if you don't have Wi-Fi, Bluetooth, a smartphone, or any other sort of high-tech connected organizer. It works with any Pocket PC.*

There's only one catch: this procedure only gets your Outlook mail. What if you have Yahoo, Hotmail, AOL, or some other Web-based e-mail account? Outlook, and by extension your Pocket PC, can't help you out.

That's where OneMail comes in. Install OneMail and you can receive all of your non-POP e-mail like Yahoo, Hotmail, and AOL on your Pocket PC in just the same way that you get your ordinary Outlook messages.

Setup is pretty simple. Run the installation software, then look for OneMail in the ActiveSync window on your desktop. If it isn't there, you'll need to turn it on manually. Choose Tools | Options from the ActiveSync menu and put a check mark next to OneMail, then click OK.

The next time you sync, you'll see a dialog box to set up at least one OneMail account. Complete the form, and those messages will be transferred to your Pocket PC. Want to add more accounts to OneMail? Just double-click the OneMail entry ActiveSync, and you can use the Add button to add extra e-mail accounts to the service.

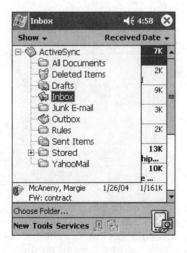

So where do you find OneMail on your Pocket PC? If you've already set things up, you may have noticed that there's no program on your Pocket PC called OneMail. That's right—to keep things simple, all your OneMail shows up in the Inbox application that comes with your PDA. Tap the Show menu and you'll see new folders that represent your other e-mail accounts.

FIND IT ON THE CD
OneMail, $29.95
Brightex Technology Limited
http://net.worth.com.hk/onemail

Send Handwritten E-Mail

Need a way to send someone a hand-drawn map? A diagram? Sketch? How about notes scribbled during a meeting? In short, wouldn't it be cool if you could e-mail someone the digital equivalent of a sticky note? That's the appeal of riteMail, a clever e-mail client for your Pocket PC.

Killer Tip *This program doesn't need any kind of wireless Internet connection, so you can use it even if you don't have Wi-Fi, Bluetooth, a smartphone, or any other sort of high-tech connected organizer. It works with any Pocket PC.*

riteMail is great for sending short notes from the road because you don't have to mess with handwriting recognition at all—just scribble with the stylus and tap Send.

To use riteMail, you first need to get a riteMail account. That's free and easy to do—just fill out the online form that pops up when you install the program. After that, just launch riteMail on your Pocket PC. Fill in your e-mail address on the User tab of the Options dialog box, and be sure to configure the Sending tab. You have two main choices on the Sending tab:

- If you want to send e-mail from your Pocket PC wirelessly, choose riteMail server from the drop-down list entitled Deliver Messages Via.

- If your Pocket PC doesn't have wireless capabilities or you'd rather send from your PC during ActiveSyncs, set the Deliver Messages Via list box to Pocket Outlook.

![riteMail settings screen]

Now you're ready to rock. Just tap the New menu at the bottom of the screen and draw, scrawl, or doodle your message. Address it and tap Send. The recipient receives a message with the image embedded in a Java window.

Killer Tip *Use the tools at the bottom of the screen to vary the colors and brushes at your disposal. The icon with the geometric shapes, for instance, tries to automatically straighten lines and turn your shapes into perfect figures like rectangles, circles, and triangles.*

FIND IT ON THE CD
riteMail, $29.95
Pen&Internet
www.ritemail.net

80 | Simple SMS

Bluetooth—Not As Ugly As It Sounds

As you've no doubt gathered by now, Bluetooth is a short-range wireless technology that allows devices to communicate with each other up to a distance of about 30 feet. That's really just a fancy way of saying that Bluetooth is a technology designed to replace connection cables. By using Bluetooth, handheld gadgets like your Pocket PC and cell phone can communicate with each other without wires and without even getting in line of sight with each other. Dave loves Bluetooth and uses it all the time—it allows him to check e-mail on his Pocket PC, for instance, while his cell phone remains discreetly tucked in his pocket.

That said, Bluetooth is a new technology that is just starting to hit the streets. That's obvious from the overall lack of "Bluetoothness" in the world; only a few Pocket PC models come with Bluetooth built in, but you can add Bluetooth to almost any PDA via a Bluetooth expansion card.

Okay, so say you have Bluetooth. What can you do with it? Here's a short list just to whet your appetite:

■ **Dial the phone** Just tap on a phone number on your Pocket PC to dial your nearby cell phone. No longer do you have to enter phone numbers separately into a cell phone address book when they're already in the PDA to begin with.

■ **Access the Internet for the Web and e-mail** Once you configure your PDA to recognize your Bluetooth cell phone, you can use your Bluetooth connection like any PDA modem to access the Internet.

■ **Print** Armed with a Bluetooth-aware printer driver, you can print to a Bluetooth-enabled desktop or portable printer. Epson, MPI Tech, and HP all sell Bluetooth adapters that work with desktop printers and portable printers.

■ **Get pictures** Now this is cool. Some Bluetooth-enabled digital cameras let you instantly, wirelessly transfer images from the camera's memory directly to your Pocket PC.

So, let's say that you are wired—err, unwired—up with Bluetooth and itching for something to do with it. Bluetooth applications are all around, but to see the power of it, you might want to start with a program like Simple SMS, which we've stuck on the CD for you.

Simple SMS lets you send and receive SMS—short text messages—via your PDA instead of your mobile phone. Why would you want to do that, you ask? Because your Pocket PC has a far larger screen and easier text entry than your phone. So leave the phone in your pocket and use your PDA instead.

When you install Simple SMS, you need to get it ready to use your phone for SMS messaging. Choose View | Options | General and make sure that the communications port is set to use Bluetooth, then tap OK. Next, choose View | Options | SMS and make sure that the check mark is set next to Use Phone Service Centre (forgive the spelling—those silly Brits). Tap OK to close.

Now you can finally send an SMS message. Choose View | New from the menu and create your message. Under the Contacts header, enter a phone number of an SMS phone that you'd like to send to and tap Add. You can add several SMS phone numbers to the list in this way, "broadcasting" the message to multiple people at once. Finally, choose Actions | Move to Outbox and Send to fire the message from your PDA through your cell phone and out into the ether.

FIND IT ON THE CD
Simple SMS, $21.00
Visual IT
www.visualit.co.uk

81 BuZZone

Wireless Icebreakers

If sending SMS messages from your PDA whets your appetite for Bluetooth, then this last program may make you start drooling all over the book. And if that happens, well, shoot—you're going to have to buy a replacement copy since this one is all wet. While you're at the bookstore, you might want to pick up a dozen or so copies and send them to all your friends.

But we digress. Here's the deal: how would you like to be able to use your PDA to find and converse with other Bluetooth-enabled geeks of the same or opposite gender? We thought you might like the sound of that. That's the idea behind BuZZone.

In a perfect world, everyone would have a Bluetooth-powered Pocket PC, and you could find friends while riding the train or hanging out in coffee shops. You'd fire up a program like BuZZone and first search for other BuZZone users, then inspect their profiles and find someone you want to chat with. Then, without ever moving out of your comfy seat, you could converse with your new friends. The reality, of course, is that precious few people will have a Pocket PC, much less a copy of BuZZone running—at least right now. Who knows? A year from now, it could be insanely popular. For now, we suggest cajoling a PDA-equipped coworker or two into installing BuZZone so you have someone to play with.

And as a plaything, BuZZone is pretty neat. When you first install it, be sure to choose Services | Profiles | My Profile and fine-tune the way you look to others.

After that, you can tap Services | Search and find other BuZZone folks. When you see someone you want to learn more about, tap and hold the pointer on the individual's icon to see his or her profile and chat.

FIND IT ON THE CD
BuZZone, $29.95
BuZZone
www.buzzone.net

Diving into Bluetooth

Ready to try your hand at Bluetooth? Once configured, it's very easy to use—but you need to begin by "pairing" the two devices that you want to communicate with each other. The pairing process is Bluetooth's built-in security. When devices are paired, both know that they have permission to communicate with each other. It's pairing that prevents you from walking down the street and connecting to a total stranger's Bluetooth device.

Typically, you'll start by pairing your Pocket PC with a mobile phone. The process varies depending upon which PDA you have, whether it includes Bluetooth, and whether you had to add Bluetooth via an add-in card. In general, here's what you do:

1. Make sure your cell phone is discoverable. You may need to read your phone's user guide to find out how to temporarily turn on its Discoverable status, but a few moments of hunting around the Settings or Bluetooth menu should turn up something pretty quickly.

2. On the PDA, find your Bluetooth settings and look for an option to connect to another device. Your PDA should search for other Bluetooth devices in the room and turn up the phone that you just made discoverable. Select the one you want to pair with.

3. Your PDA will ask you for a passkey or pairing code. Enter the code into the Pocket PC, and then, in order to pair the devices, your phone will immediately ask you to reenter that code.

You should be able to use the devices together now. If you were configuring your PDA to use a phone to connect to the Internet, you might have an extra step or two. You might be asked, for instance, to enter the phone number that the Pocket PC should dial to access the Internet. Check with your wireless provider for that information.

Chapter 8

A Penny Saved

  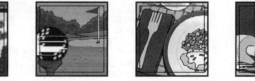

See if this scenario sounds familiar: Right around April 10, you figure it's time to start putting the old tax return together. To your horror, you discover that your records of the year gone by consist of a drawer full of crumpled receipts, scribbled expense reports, and unrecognized bank statements.

Doesn't sound like you? Okay, try this on for size: the check you just wrote at Sam's Club is going to bounce because you didn't know your account was overdrawn. Or this: your company won't reimburse you for the convention in Anaheim because you didn't keep adequate records of your expenses.

Whether you're "challenged" at managing your finances or simply looking for more efficient methods, Pocket PC software developers have plenty of solutions. We've gathered some great programs designed to help you track, organize, and manage everything from checking accounts to stock portfolios.

82 Stock Manager

Stock Your PDA with Your Stock Portfolio

Anyone who plays the stock market knows that information is often the most valuable asset. TinyStocks' Stock Manager brings information straight to your PDA, thereby enabling you to keep tabs on your portfolio even when you're out and about.

Name	Price	Profit	
Adobe	29.52	1186.05 ↓
AMD	20.74	259.05 ↓
AOL	35.15	103.05 ↑
Applied Mat...	37.8125	664.43 ↓
IBM	92	1900.00 ↑
Intel	22.625	-288.70 ↓
JDS Uniphase	13.734...	92.08 ↓
Microsoft	51.9375	2873.80 ↓
Nokia	22.30	330.00 ↑
Nortel	12.96	218.45 ↑ ▯
Sun	13.86	331.65 ↓

Profit:	7669.85		
Profit %:	35.44%	Cost:	21640.63
Profit PA:	69.96%	Value:	29310.49

This is a robust piece of software. It enables you to manage an unlimited number of stocks across multiple portfolios. It supports different currencies and can alert you when it detects critical changes (such as price, profit, daily change, and so on) in any of your stocks. Most importantly, it updates your portfolio every time you ActiveSync, downloading the latest info via your computer's Internet connection. This info includes current stock price; the day's high, low, change, volume, bid, and ask; and 52-week high/low values. Stock Manager also provides valuable at-a-glance reference tools such as pie, bar, and line charts, so you can monitor your monetary distribution and stock-price histories.

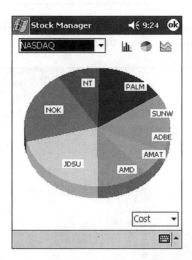

   If you're lucky enough to own a wireless PDA—one that connects to the Internet via cellular service, Wi-Fi, or even Bluetooth—you can download market updates anywhere there's a live connection. That could come in mighty handy if, say, you're stuck in a meeting and tracking a volatile stock. Thankfully, TinyStocks doesn't charge extra for a subscription—the price of the software includes unlimited lifetime updates.

Killer Tip   *Buy low, sell high. Just kidding—you probably already know that one. But if you're relatively new to the stock market or just need some investment strategies, pay a visit to the Motley Fool (www.fool.com). The site's mission: "To educate, enrich, and amuse individual investors around the world." How enriched you become is ultimately up to you, but the site definitely delivers on the education and amusement fronts.*

FIND IT ON THE CD
Stock Manager, $24.95
TinyStocks
www.tinystocks.com

83 Mastersoft Money

Manage Your Money on Your Pocket PC

Mastersoft Money may be the greatest finance-management program in history that doesn't synchronize with Microsoft Money or Quicken, the two top finance-management

POWER APP

programs for PCs. In fact, it doesn't synchronize with any desktop software—it's just a stand-alone money manager, and a darn good one at that.

The interface is both attractive and uncluttered, with icons providing single-tap access to the program's seven primary functions. You can track multiple accounts, define categories for your income and expenses, and record transactions in a simplistic register. The software can generate an amazing variety of reports, graphs, and charts, covering everything from P&L to net worth.

While Mastersoft Money was designed to be a stand-alone finance manager, it's not completely cut off from the desktop. It can import and export QIF files, which are compatible with Quicken and Microsoft Money. Thus, it's possible to, say, import your desktop Quicken data for review, or to export your Mastersoft Money records and view them in Microsoft Money. This is something of a hassle, to be sure—if you want to synchronize directly with your desktop money manager, you may want to look at another program.

Pocket Quicken (www.landware.com), for instance, is a mobile edition of the desktop classic. It lets you record your transactions on the spot, and then updates your desktop records when you synchronize. It works the other way, too, so you're always carrying up-to-date account information. Memorized transactions and auto-completing fields are among the included Quicken amenities, and a PIN protects your data from potentially prying eyes. You can find the demo on the CD!

Microsoft Money users will want to check out Microsoft's own mobile companion, Money 2003 for Pocket PC (www.microsoft.com/windowsmobile/resources/ downloads/pocketpc/money.mspx). As with Quicken, Money 2003 copies and receives data when you ActiveSync, so you're always carrying your current financial picture. Money 2003 also downloads portfolio information so you can check the performance of your stocks. Best of all, this little sidekick is a freebie. Find it on the CD!

If you're not already tied to a desktop finance program, however, Mastersoft Money could be the only money manager you'll ever need.

Killer Tip *If you use Mastersoft Money or Pocket Quicken to manage business expenses, it qualifies as a business expense. Therefore, you should be able to deduct the purchase come tax time. Of course, we're not H&R Block, so check with your financial advisor to make sure.*

FIND IT ON THE CD

Mastersoft Money, $29.95
Mastersoft Mobile Solutions
www.mastersoftmobilesolutions.com

---

84 Rebate Information Tracker

Keep Tabs on Those Rebates

To Rick, the only words sweeter than "after rebate" are "free after rebate." These days, rebate deals are everywhere, from your local drugstore to your local electronics superstore to Amazon.com. For the cost of an envelope and a postage stamp, you can reclaim some serious coin on a variety of purchases.

The problem lies in managing—and especially tracking—these rebates. In most cases, it takes six to eight weeks to receive your check. Unless you're one of those highly organized types, you're likely to forget which checks have arrived, when you sent in the forms, and so on. You may even forget to send the forms at all, or decide it's not worth the hassle for five or ten bucks. That's more or less what product vendors are hoping will happen—don't let them win!

Enter Rebate Information Tracker, a simple program designed to, well, track rebate information. It's a very basic tool, offering exactly six fields to store rebate data: product name, store, price, rebate amount, date purchased, and date rebate sent. Unfortunately, it doesn't offer a notes field or anyplace else to record things like contact numbers or web addresses. And when a rebate finally arrives, you have to delete the record—you can't just checkmark it. The good news is, Rebate Information Tracker is free, so if it doesn't meet your needs, you're not out any cash.

Killer Tip *If you like the idea behind Rebate Information Tracker but need to store more information about your rebates, you may be better off setting up a simple spreadsheet in Pocket Excel. Better yet, design the spreadsheet in Excel on your PC, then convert it to Pocket Excel on your Pocket PC. Of course, now you're wondering why you need your Pocket PC at all if you've got a rebate-tracking spreadsheet on your PC. Good point!*

FIND IT ON THE CD
Rebate Information Tracker, Free
Binh Ho
www.handango.com

85 | Financial Analyzer

Pocket-Friendly Financial Planning

The only thing Rick is worse at than managing money is math. Hence his appreciation for PocketSoftWear.com's Financial Analyzer, which offers a set of useful financial-calculation worksheets for things like loan payments, amortization, asset depreciation, cash-flow analysis, and so on.

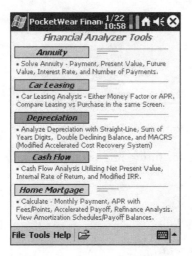

The software's interface is admirably simple, starting with a home screen that divides the worksheets into five categories: Annuity, Car Leasing, Depreciation, Cash Flow, and Home Mortgage. Within each section are worksheets for accomplishing various calculations. Home Mortgage, for instance, includes options like Monthly Payment, Accelerated Payoff, and Refinance Analyzer. The latter is one example of how the program can pay for itself in one use. In addition to calculating the monthly savings that come from refinancing, it factors in all manner of added costs, such as application fees, title insurance, and the like. Thus, you can find out just how much you're saving by refinancing and instantly determine if it's a worthwhile move. The software can also generate an amortization schedule.

Killer Tip *Financial Analyzer doesn't include a pop-up calendar for fields that require you to enter a date. Use the format DD/MM/YY. If you need help understanding certain finance-related terms, tap Help | Finance Glossary for a listing of terms and definitions.*

The ability to quickly and easily crunch these kinds of numbers can come in mighty handy when you're haggling with a car salesman or working with a mortgage lender. Not only can you check the figures to make sure they're accurate, you can look at endless what-if scenarios without relying on someone else's math.

Our only complaint with the program is that you can't export any of the calculations for printing or review on your PC. You can, however, save data sets on your Pocket PC for future reference.

FIND IT ON THE CD
Financial Analyzer, $29.99
PocketSoftWear.com
www.pocketsoftwear.com

86 | Car Loan Calculator

Dude, Can I Afford That Car?

Some programs fall squarely into the Just Plain Handy category. Car Loan Calculator (see Figure 8-1) is one of them. True to its name, this simple but elegant number cruncher lets you calculate payments on new and used cars. It factors in things like registration fees, down payments, rebates, trade-in credits, and so on.

Helpful as this can be for the prospective buyer, it's also a valuable tool for car salespeople. You can give customers ballpark car-payment estimates, which undoubtedly look a lot more honest on the Pocket PC screen than the figures you scribble on a piece of paper after furiously mashing a calculator.

For the record, you could buy Financial Analyzer ("Pocket-Friendly Financial Planning"). It does car leasing/payment calculations as well. However, it costs six times more than Car Loan Calculator, and the latter is a lot more user-friendly.

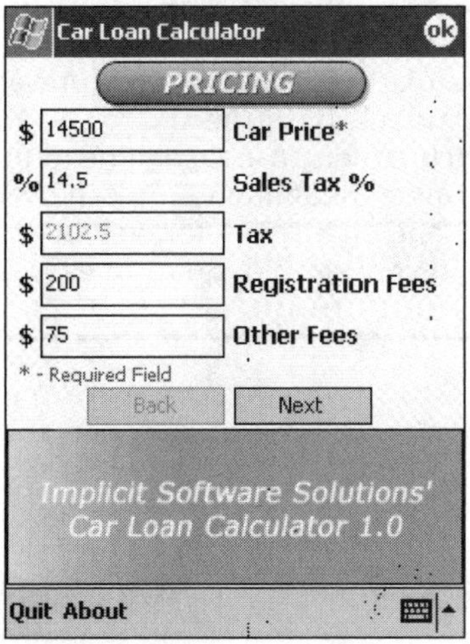

FIGURE 8-1   With Car Loan Calculator, you can quickly and easily determine the monthly payments for any loan—without all the funny stuff dealers throw at you.

Killer Tip *Looking for car-buying tips? Want to avoid the ten most common dealer scams? You can find both at www.carbuyingtips.com.*

FIND IT ON THE CD
Car Loan Calculator, $4.95
Implicit Software Solutions
www.implicitsoftware.com

Keep Your Screen Pristine

A scratched screen is the bane of every PDA user. But with all the grit, paper clips, and other flotsam floating around your pocket or purse, scratches can be hard to avoid. That's why we strongly recommend some kind of screen protection. Yes, a good case goes a long way, but it's not enough. For maximum insurance, you need a plastic covering that adheres directly to the LCD.

Although there are many choices available (your local office-supply or computer superstore should carry a decent selection), we're partial to ClearTouch (www.boxwave.com), a glare-reducing, scratch-preventing sheet that's available for virtually all Pocket PC models (visit the site to see a complete list). Unlike most screen protectors, which are disposable and need to be replaced every month or so, ClearTouch lasts almost indefinitely. You can even remove, clean, and reapply it. Rick's had the same one on his PDA for well over a year, and it's still in good condition. (But for the record, it's not quite so easy to apply the second time.)

Chapter 9

And Finally, Our Favorites

T his chapter is something of a catchall, a place to spotlight loads of great products that don't necessarily fit in other categories. In these pages you'll learn how to pack news, weather, movie show times, and more onto your Pocket PC's Today screen—and make it look good in the process. You'll augment the stock Pocket PC calendar with one that offers a much more appealing month-at-a-glance view. You'll read e-books the way they were meant to be read. And you'll replace Windows Media Player with one of the coolest MP3 players we've ever seen. Ah, your PDA—it just gives and gives and gives...

87 | Journal Bar

Pack Your Today Screen with News and Notables

POWER APP

Quite possibly the best thing ever to happen to your Pocket PC's Today screen, Omega One's Journal Bar packs it with news headlines, stock quotes, weather forecasts, sports scores, movie times, TV listings, and plenty more—all customized based on your zip code and personal preferences.

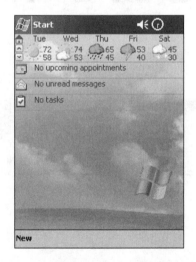

Reminiscent of AvantGo (see Chapter 7), the software downloads data via your PC's Internet connection when you synchronize. It occupies just three lines in the Today screen (and you can position it to your liking), so it doesn't overwhelm the space. Using a pair of arrows, you scroll between "banks" of information: news, weather, stocks, and so on. Tapping any entry takes you to another screen—usually Internet

Explorer—for a more complete listing. The $9.99 purchase price includes free lifetime updates, making Journal Bar an exceptional bargain.

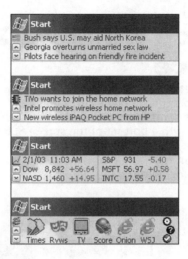

Installing and using Journal Bar couldn't be easier. After it's loaded on your Pocket PC, just enter your ZIP code (a one-time task) and ActiveSync (making sure your computer is online). The software downloads its default channels, a process that happens entirely behind the scenes. In fact, it's a bit tricky to know when the updates are occurring and when they're complete. But it usually takes no more than a minute or two. Just make sure your computer is online when you sync.

Killer Tip *You can use Journal Bar to download just about any web link and view those pages offline. To set this up, scroll through Journal Bar's pages until you see the one with the little red bull's-eye in the corner. Tap it, then tap Journal Bar, Options, and then the Links tab. Replace the fifth or sixth item with the link of your choice. The next time you ActiveSync, Journal Bar will fetch that page. Keep in mind, however, that it retrieves only the linked page, not any subsequent links within that page. Thus, if you connect to a site such as www.engadget.com, you'll see only the info on that home page. If you tap one of the links, you'll get an error (unless you have a wireless Internet connection, that is).*

FIND IT ON THE CD
Journal Bar, $14.99
Omega One
www.omegaone.com

88 eXPerience

Experience Windows XP with eXPerience

The Windows CE, Pocket PC, and Windows Mobile operating systems have all represented Microsoft's effort to shoehorn Windows into a handheld PC. For better or worse, Digital Expedition's eXPerience transforms the stock interface into the spitting image of Windows XP, complete with a bottom-of-the-screen Start button, fly-out menus, and instant access to frequently and recently used programs. It replaces the Today screen with up to nine program icons (you can switch back to Today with a single tap) and enables you to close running programs with ease.

It's ironic that a utility designed to add familiarity to the interface brings such complexity along with it. You have to navigate some fairly confusing setup screens to pin programs to the Start menu or add icons to the desktop—no context-sensitive tap-and-hold options here. Fortunately, you can find a thorough instruction manual in the eXPerience install folder on your desktop. It's also available here: www.digitalexpedition.com/main/eXPerience/eSupport/help2/help.html.

Once you have eXPerience configured to your liking and wrap your brain around using XP on a PDA, it's pretty darn cool. Purty, too.

Killer Tip   *You don't have to keep the Start menu at the bottom of the screen. If you're already accustomed to having it up top, but still want to use eXPerience's interface, just use its docking feature (also borrowed from Windows XP, by the way). Just tap and hold anywhere on the desktop, then choose Properties from the pop-up menu. Tap the Dock tab, then choose your desired spot for the Start menu.*

FIND IT ON THE CD
eXPerience, $19.99
Digital Expedition
www.digitalexpedition.com

89 Explorer 2003

An Intrepid "Explorer"

If there's a more unintuitive and underpowered file manager than Microsoft's File Explorer for Pocket PC, we've yet to discover it. resco's Explorer 2003 is exactly the opposite, a logical and powerful file manager that you'll soon wish Microsoft had the sense to adopt for the Pocket PC operating system.

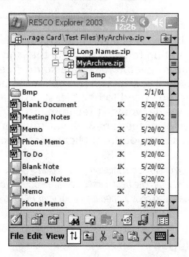

It starts with a split-screen folder view, which makes for easy file discovery and relocation. You can copy, move, compress (using the Zip format), beam, transmit via Bluetooth (but only on iPAQs), print, and encrypt (using beefy algorithms) your files.

Explorer 2003 also includes an image viewer, a search function (hel-*lo*!), and even a Registry editor, for particularly advanced users.

The Explorer 2003 interface is clean and logically laid out, though you might need to consult the documentation to learn what all the icons do. (Why do developers never add little text descriptors? It would make life *so* much easier.) resco's documentation is thorough, but could stand a few more screenshots to help novices get their bearings.

Speaking of novices, you need to be at least an intermediate user to really reap Explorer 2003's benefits—we wouldn't recommend it for beginners, who generally don't need to manage a lot of files anyway. But for everyone else, they should call it Rescue Explorer, as it saves you from Microsoft's wimpy file manager.

Killer Tip *Running out of storage space on your Pocket PC? Use Explorer 2003's Zip capability to compress infrequently used files. The best candidates are Pocket Word and Pocket Excel files, BMP images, and other raw data. You can also copy zipped files from your PC and expand them on your Pocket PC.*

FIND IT ON THE CD
Explorer 2003, $19.95
resco
www.resco-net.com

90 | SuperCalendar

Look, Up in the Sky...It's SuperCalendar!

If you rely heavily on your Pocket PC calendar and want a turbocharged alternative, you could install something like Agenda Fusion (see Chapter 5) or Pocket Informant (www.pocketinformant.com). But those are heavyweight suites that replace other core apps as well. SuperCalendar replaces just the calendar—but how super is it?

For one thing, it costs quite a bit less than the suites—just $9.95. The program's modus operandi is to give you an enriched month-at-a-glance view, one with timelines, icons, and as much or as little color-coding as you prefer. There's definite value in this, as the anemic month view tends to be a chief complaint among users switching to PDAs from paper planners. With SuperCalendar, you can quickly and easily spot all-day events (represented by a red line spanning the timeline), days that are light or busy, and icon-worthy events like travel and business meetings.

If you tap and hold your stylus on any day in the calendar, a pop-up window lists the day's events. A quick tap, conversely, takes you to a different screen with a more complete list. It's still just text, but here you can modify appointments (via the standard form) by double-tapping.

While SuperCalendar makes it easy to navigate from month to month—they span the top of the screen—we'd like the program even better if it had day and week views. In other words, the month-at-a-glance overhaul is great, but where's the visual day-at-a-glance? Plus, SuperCalendar's icons are something of a mixed bag. Only three can fit in a day's slot (so you might "miss out" on important ones), and they don't appear in the pop-up or daily summaries.

Still, for just ten bucks, SuperCalendar could be just the ticket for users who need a better month-view calendar than what the Pocket PC OS provides.

Killer Tip *A good companion product for use with SuperCalendar is Calendar Plus Today (www.sbsh.net), which shows your upcoming tasks and appointments (up to 30 days' worth) right on your Today screen. This little gem sells for $8.99; a trial version is available at the company's web site.*

FIND IT ON THE CD
SuperCalendar, $9.95
ScaryBear Software
www.scarybearsoftware.com

91 Palm Reader

Read It or Weep!

Palm Reader enables you to read electronic books (e-books) on your Pocket PC. "Whoa," you're thinking, "stop right there, you smarty-pants authors. Pocket PCs already come with Microsoft Reader, right? Isn't *that* an e-book reader? And isn't *Palm* Reader a *Palm* program? What's this all about? Explain yourselves!"

Settle down there, cowpoke. Yes, Palm Reader was born a Palm OS product, but it has since been ported to Pocket PC. And we think it's a much better e-book reader than Microsoft Reader, for reasons that'll become evident starting in the very next sentence. For starters, we've tried Microsoft Reader, and we're not wild about it. It's extremely awkward to use, and it doesn't even use the entire screen—there's a white border around the text that results in fewer words fitting on each "page."

Palm Reader has no such border, meaning you needn't flip pages quite so often. And speaking of which, you can flip pages just by tapping on the top half (to go back) or bottom half (to go forward) of the screen. Better still, Palm Reader has none of the digital rights management (DRM) hassles of Microsoft Reader. If you want to "loan" a book to a friend or family member, you can just beam it right to their PDA. (You'll also have to give them the credit card number you used to buy the book, which we think is a smart method of copy protection.)

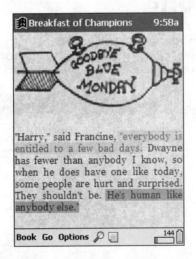

As for Palm Digital Media, the site is home to thousands of fiction and nonfiction e-books, from *The Da Vinci Code* to *The 7 Habits of Highly Effective People*. They're all discounted, though not as much as we think they should be. (E-books cost nothing to print and next to nothing to distribute.)

Killer Tip   *You can save an extra 10 percent on each e-book purchase by subscribing to the Palm Digital Media newsletter. It comes via e-mail once per week and includes a discount code you enter at the time of purchase.*

In closing, if you've never read a book on your PDA, you should try it. Skeptics often balk at the idea, thinking the screen is too small or it's just too weird. Hey, they said the same thing about television. Rick is a huge fan of e-books and carries a few on his handheld at all times. That way, there's always something good to read, no matter where you are.

92 StartPad

Put Your Program Icons Where They Belong

It can take two, three, sometimes even four taps just to start a program on a Pocket PC. That's because most program icons are buried in the Start menu. Stellarmetrics' gee-why-didn't-Microsoft-think-of-that StartPad puts icons for your favorite applications right on the Today screen, where all it takes is a single tap to start a program.

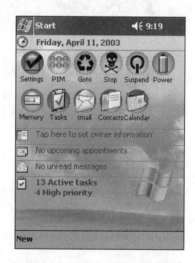

StartPad can also display icons for useful system tools, such as memory and battery status, application shutdown, and so on. It can even automatically switch between "work" and "play" configurations depending on the time of day, so your business apps appear during office hours, your fun stuff after hours.

It's kind of a hassle to add your own icon choices to the Today screen—you actually have to copy and paste them between folders—but that's a small price to pay for this kind of convenience.

Killer Tip *As of press time, Stellarmetrics' web site seemed to be down, and our e-mails to the company were returned as undeliverable. However, StartPad is still available for purchase from Handango (www.handango.com), and it's inexpensive and practical enough that we still think it's worth owning. Buyer beware, however—if the company doesn't emerge from limbo, you won't have any support for the product.*

FIND IT ON THE CD
StartPad, $7.50
Stellarmetrics
www.stellarmetrics.com, www.handango.com

93 Battery Pack

Give Your Today Screen the Royal Treatment

If Journal Bar (see "Pack Your Today Screen with News and Notables," earlier in this chapter) is the best thing ever to happen to your Pocket PC's Today screen, Battery Pack is undoubtedly the second best. Don't be fooled by the name: although this program offers a very nifty battery gauge, it also does a lot more. For instance, it outfits your Today screen with one-tap shortcuts to frequently used programs. It puts a screen-brightness control right where you can get at it. And it displays all manner of memory and storage-card information. It is, in short, the way the Today screen should work.

Battery Pack adds two main "bars"—rows of icons, essentially—to your Today screen. The Program Bar contains eight quick-launch buttons you can customize to your liking (use this for favorite programs and functions) and a row of program icons for every program installed on your Pocket PC. Can't identify a program from its icon? Just tap and hold to find out what it is. Too many programs to fit on one line? Tap the scroll arrows to roll up additional rows of icons.

The Battery Bar shows battery life, available memory, and available space on your primary storage card. It also includes backlight and screen-brightness controls—the latter worth the price of admission by itself (as it saves you endless taps navigating your way to the Pocket PC's own brightness settings).

The handy features don't end there. Battery Pack will inform you—not with beeps or flashes, but with spoken words—when you're running out of storage space or your battery is low or fully charged. Its Power Clean feature removes unnecessary files to free memory, while Power Light effectively turns the Pocket PC into a flashlight (a white screen with maximum brightness—handier than you might think).

In short, we'd say that if you install only one of our 101 killer apps on your Pocket PC, make it this one. It is single-handedly the most useful tool we've ever used.

Killer Tip *If your Pocket PC seems to act sluggish after you run a few programs, take advantage of Battery Pack's Power Task feature. Tap the little down-arrow in the top-right corner of the screen, and then tap Close All But Active. This will shut down performance-hogging programs that are still running.*

FIND IT ON THE CD
Battery Pack, $19.99
Omega One
www.omegaone.com

94 PocketMusic

Pocket Your Music

Sure, Windows Media Player is capable of playing MP3 and WMA audio files, but it's not the prettiest program around (or even the most intuitive). That's why we're partial to PocketMusic, a robust music player that's notable not just for how it works, but also for how it looks. Here's a shot of the program as it normally appears:

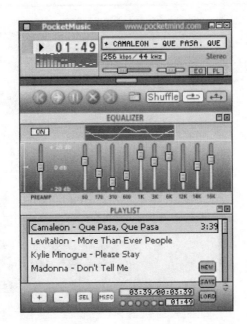

And here are a few examples of the skins you can download to change
PocketMusic's appearance:

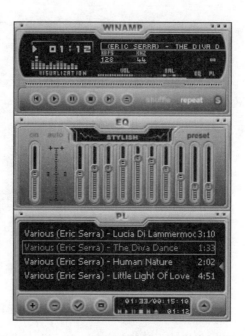

If these look a bit familiar, you're probably a Winamp user. Winamp is a mega-popular MP3 player for Windows, one that's compatible with thousands of user-designed custom skins. Those same skins are compatible with PocketMusic, so you can choose just about any look or theme you like. (Actually, the software supports skins created for Winamp 2.*x*—those designed for later versions won't work.) It also supports playlists created with Winamp—very handy if you've already created a bunch. Okay, you twisted our arms, here's one more example skin:

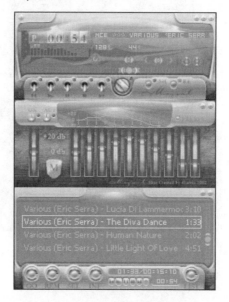

PocketMusic supports not only MP3 and unprotected WMA files, but also the increasingly popular Ogg Vorbis format. (If you have to ask what that is, you might as well stick with MP3s.) It includes a ten-band equalizer with nearly two dozen presets, an extra-bass feature, a landscape mode with oversize buttons (ideal if you use your Pocket PC to play tunes in your car), and a battery-saving option that turns off the screen (while the player keeps playing). Our favorite feature of all is bookmarks, an indispensable tool for anyone who listens to audio books or other lengthy audio files (see the discussion of Replay Radio in Chapter 3 for information on recording Internet radio—bookmarks come in very handy for those kinds of programs).

Another great PocketMusic perk is the alarm option, which turns your Pocket PC into a poor person's—make that cool person's—clock radio. Just set your desired wakeup time and choose a tune, and PocketMusic will play it when it "goes off."

If there's a downside to PocketMusic, it's the somewhat confusing interface. If you're adept with Winamp, you should feel right at home. Everyone else should spend some time perusing Guide-PMBundle.doc, a Word-formatted instruction manual located in the Zip file containing the program. It covers the basics, but it'll probably take some fiddling with the program before you're comfortable with it. We're not novices when it comes to this stuff, but even we had trouble figuring out certain features.

Killer Tip   *By default, PocketMusic occupies your entire Pocket PC screen. To access the program's options, tap the little square in the top-left corner. An even better tip: to copy audio files to your memory card, pop it into your PC's media reader (if you have one). You'll get the job done much faster than if you use ActiveSync's Explore window.*

It's worth noting that there's a freeware version of PocketMusic that works quite well—it just lacks some of the more advanced features, like skins, WMA support, equalizer presets, and mappable hardware buttons.

95 PocketPC Mark

How Fast Is This PDA, Anyway?

Calling all geeks, power users, and overclockers (you know who you are): If you're not happy until you know exactly how fast (or slow) your Pocket PC is performing, until you have raw numbers proving your PDA is the speediest one on the block, have we got a program for you. It's called PocketPC Mark, and it runs seven separate benchmarks to gauge various areas of performance.

Play Music-Service Downloads on Your Pocket PC

Music services like iTunes, MusicMatch, and Napster have made it possible to buy songs and albums for a reasonable price and keep your conscience guilt-free at the same time. However, nifty as these services are, they're annoyingly limited in one key way: the songs you buy can't be played on some Pocket PCs, owing to DRM restrictions. Even though many services sell songs in the WMA format, which is supported by both PocketMusic and Windows Media Player, their DRM licenses prohibit playback on many portable devices. (Actually, if your Pocket PC runs the Windows Mobile 2003 operating system, you can indeed play DRM-protected WMA files.)

Fortunately, there's an easy—and legal—solution. Just burn your songs to a CD, then "rip" them back to your PC in MP3 format. (MusicMatch is one of many programs that can perform this function—visit www.download.com to find others.) Yes, it's a bit of a hassle, but it gets the job done. This will work regardless of whether you use iTunes, Napster, or another service (provided it permits you to burn CDs—virtually all of them do). Once you've converted the songs to MP3 format, just copy them to your Pocket PC and play them in your preferred player. Take that, greedy record companies!

(Audiophiles, take note: this conversion from WMA to CD to MP3 results in a slight reduction in sound quality, though it takes a keen ear to detect it.)

A *benchmark,* in case you're not familiar with the term, is essentially a speed test. PocketPC Mark includes two different CPU tests, two memory tests, and one each for graphics, storage cards, and the file system. The storage-card test is particularly valuable, as it can help you determine whether the "32x" SD Card you paid extra for is really any faster than its standard-speed cousin. (Have patience, though—the storage-card test is really slow, taking upwards of an hour to complete.) And all the tests will reveal your device's performance relative to other PDAs, so you not only can see how it measures up, but also determine if something's slowing you down.

Installing PocketPC Mark is a bit different than installing other programs. The Zip file contains four different versions of the utility—you have to choose the one that's compatible with your Pocket PC model. PocketPCMark_MIPS.exe and PocketPCMark_SH3.exe, for instance, work only with older devices, those that use MIPS and SH3 processors, respectively. PocketPCMark_ARM.exe is for models that use ARM

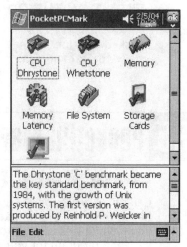

processors, like the HP Jornada and Compaq iPAQ 36xx series. Most users will want PocketPCMark_ARM_PPC2002.exe, which is compatible with devices using the Pocket PC 2002 and Windows Mobile 2003 operating systems (all of which use ARM processors).

To install PocketPC Mark, you must manually copy the proper EXE file to your handheld. Here's how:

1. Double-click the pocketpcmark.zip file to open it.

2. Place your Pocket PC in its cradle, wait for it to finish synchronizing, then open the ActiveSync window on your computer.

3. Click the Explore icon in ActiveSync. A Mobile Device window opens.

4. Drag PocketPCMark_ARM_PPC2002.exe (or whichever file is appropriate for your Pocket PC model) from the Zip window to the Mobile Device window. You'll see a new window indicating the copy progress. When it's done, so are you!

To run PocketPC Mark, tap Start | Programs | File Explorer, then navigate to the My Documents folder. You should see a PocketPCMark program icon. Tap it to get started. When you tap once on any of the benchmark icons, you'll see a description and/or history in the window below. That's one of the things we really like about this program.

Killer Tip *Load PocketPC Mark on a memory card. That way, you can easily move it from one Pocket PC to another for quick comparisons of their performance. On the other hand, if you're planning to use it to measure memory card speed, you'll want to copy it from the card to the Pocket PC's internal RAM.*

FIND IT ON THE CD
PocketPC Mark, $6.95
Anton Tomov
www.antontomov.com

96 Pocket Earth

Put the Earth in Your Pocket

In Neal Stephenson's novel *Snow Crash,* Hiro Protagonist uses a virtual 3-D globe in the Mateaverse to access all of the Central Intelligence Corporation's worldwide intelligence data. Now, with Pocket Earth, you can have your own virtual Earth on your Pocket PC.

While it isn't packed with CIC intelligence data, Pocket Earth is pretty cool nonetheless. It's designed to duplicate all of the benefits of having a real world globe right on your PDA, and then some. Pocket Earth renders a stunningly beautiful rendition of the world on your screen, spinning as you watch. It re-creates the day/night terminator and illuminates nighttime cities as if you were seeing them from space.

Pocket Earth's features are extensive. You can spin and zoom in or out of the globe for a better view of any location, and get detailed information about any of the program's 15,000 cities just by clicking on the appropriate spot. Want to find Baltimore in a hurry? There's a pop-up search box for finding specific cities. You can see local time, sunrise and sunset information, and more on any selected locale. Want to know the distance from Denver to New York via Chicago? You can construct a simple route between two cities or a complex one between two dozen, and see total distance instantly.

Killer Tip   *Blue Point Studio offers a collection of add-on maps as well. You can turn Pocket Earth into the Moon or Mars, for instance, and overlay maps let you see the Earth with political boundaries or realistically fluffy clouds—all free downloads.*

Pocket Earth is one of those showpiece applications that you whip out to impress your non-PDA-carrying friends. Even if you don't have a recurring need to find the sunset time in Zhob, we suspect this is a program you'll want to buy for your Pocket PC. It's just that impressive.

FIND IT ON THE CD
Pocket Earth, $14.95
Blue Point Studio
www.bluepointstudio.com

97 GeoKron

In Australia, It's Already Yesterday

GeoKron—it sounds like a doomsday weapon Kirk would have to race against time to defeat in *Star Trek*. In reality, GeoKron involves neither Kirk nor doomsday, but it does have a lot to do with time. It's a sophisticated world clock, one that shows you the local time in over 500 cities across the planet, which is attractively illustrated on your screen. It also shows you where it's daytime and nighttime.

Built with frequent travelers in mind, GeoKron also includes airport codes and area codes for cities around the world. It has an alarm-clock feature that lets you set alarms not just for your time zone, but for any other. Thus, suppose you need to call someone at 3 P.M. Rome time, but you're in Cedar Rapids. Just tap Tools | Alarms, then specify the time, place, and day.

Need to know the distance between, say, Ann Arbor and Baton Rouge? GeoKron's distance calculator tells you not only the mileage, but the time it takes to travel based on various modes of transportation (from hoofing it to taking the train to flying on a commercial jet). With a few more taps, you can get sunrise or moonrise information for any city in GeoKron's database.

One thing we particularly like about GeoKron is its built-in "program tour," which walks you through using the software and explains certain features. When you first start the program, tap the link that says "Click here to start your tour of GeoKron." (You can return to it at anytime from within the program by tapping Settings | About GeoKron, and then tapping the yellow question mark in the corner of the screen. Then, tap View | Contents.)

You can even add GeoKron's world clock to your Today screen. If you didn't choose this option during setup, tap Start | Settings | Today, then tap the Items tab and check the box next to GeoKron.

Killer Tip *Want to add a city to GeoKron's database? You can, though it's not the most intuitive process. Tap Settings | Edit Cities, and then tap Copy. This will create a copy of whatever city is selected. You can then go in and modify the city name, country, airport code, and so on. When you tap OK, GeoKron will ask you if you want to save the new city. Tap Yes and you're off to the races.*

FIND IT ON THE CD

GeoKron, $12.95
Vistasoft, Inc.
www.geokron.com

98 Remote Display Control for Pocket PC

Remote Possibilities

In Chapter 3, you learned to use your Pocket PC as a remote control. In this section, we're going to show you how to remotely control your Pocket PC. Why would you want to do that? Suppose you want to train a group of people in how to use a Pocket PC, or you need to make a business presentation that involves one in some way. With Microsoft's Remote Display Control (RDC), your Pocket PC effectively runs in a window on your desktop PC or notebook (see Figure 9-1). Actions performed on the PC are reflected on the PDA, and vice versa.

If you have a notebook connected to a business projector, you now have the opportunity to interact with and demonstrate a Pocket PC in real time. The only tricky part is getting this handy utility up and running. Here's how:

1. Run the RemoteDSP.exe program contained on the CD. It will install RDC on your PC and Pocket PC.

2. While your Pocket PC is still in its cradle, click the Start button on your computer, then click All Programs | Remote Display Control | Remote Display Control Host. This launches the PC side of the application.

3. On your Pocket PC, tap Start | Programs | cerdisp. Tap Connect, after which you'll see a box requesting a Hostname. It should read PPP_PEER, which is normal. Tap OK, and in a moment you should see a "live" Pocket PC image on your PC.

4. Now you can interact with your Pocket PC using your computer's mouse as a surrogate stylus (remember to click just once instead of twice). You can even use the keyboard to enter data.

 FIGURE 9-1   No, this isn't your Pocket PC. Well, actually, it is, but you're seeing it in Windows on a desktop system.

That's pretty darn cool. And did we mention Remote Display Control is a freebie?

Killer Tip *RDC is one of Microsoft's so-called Power Toys—programs and utilities that extend your PDA's capabilities. Although it's not like Microsoft to give things away, all Power Toys are free. However, they're also unsupported, use-at-your-own-risk programs. (For the record, we've never encountered a problem with any of them.) Other Power Toys include an expense tracker and a theme generator (including a Today-screen plug-in that will automatically switch themes at designated intervals). You can find them all at the same URL for RDC.*

FIND IT ON THE CD

Remote Display Control for Pocket PC, Free
Microsoft
www.microsoft.com/windowsmobile/resources/downloads/pocketpc/powertoys.mspx

99 Dose-A-Day

Get Your Daily Dose of *Dilbert* (or Golf)

Much as we're fond of those tear-off calendars that reveal a new joke, historical fact, or surgery tip every day, they sure do waste paper. Not so Dose-A-Day calendars, which give you a daily helping of Close to Home (a *Far Side*–like comic), *Dilbert,* or golf.

These nifty calendars can be set to appear every time you turn on your PDA, the first time you turn it on each day, or at a specified time. Unlike a traditional paper calendar, Dose-A-Day doesn't start January 1—it starts whenever you install it, so you invariably get 365 days' worth of material. You can revisit missed days and even store your favorite pages, but you can't skip ahead—a smart preventative measure against those who can't help peeking.

Dose-A-Day's memory requirements vary, from about 500KB for Golf to 1.3MB for *Dilbert*. That's pretty steep, and unfortunately the software won't run from memory cards. Still, these are ideal gifts for your favorite PDA user, yourself included.

FIND IT ON THE CD
Dose-A-Day, $19.95
DataViz
www.dataviz.com

Multiple Personality Disorder

Some kinds of multiple personality disorders, like the one that plagues Dave (look, he's Will Smith! He's Jeff Bridges! He's Ben Stiller! Oh, right, he just *wishes* he were those people—sad, really), are bad. Other kinds, like the TodayX variety, are good. This nifty utility lets you switch between four different Today screens with nothing more than the tap of your stylus.

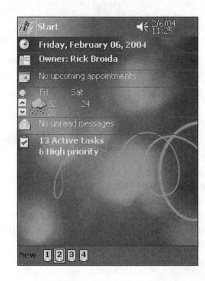

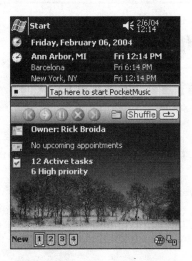

Why would you want four different Today screens? Well, how about one that's tailored to work and another to play? One that includes Battery Pack and Journal Bar, another with GeoKron and PocketMusic? (You couldn't easily fit all four of these cool programs on the same Today screen.) TodayX gives you four Today screens to customize to your liking, and not just in terms of their content—you can also choose a different theme for each screen.

Killer Tip *New to the idea of themes? By definition, a theme is a color scheme and background image for your Today screen. There are zillions of user- and even professionally designed themes out there for the download. A great place to find them is PocketPC Themes (www.pocketpcthemes.com). If you really want to get fancy, you can install animated themes that make your Today screen come alive (figuratively speaking, of course). Find the Animated Today program at www.gigabytesol.com.*

One caveat regarding TodayX: it's a little slow. On our iPAQ H3850—an older model, admittedly—it took about five seconds to switch between Today screens. Doesn't sound like much, but in PDA time it's an eternity. TodayX will likely perform better on newer Pocket PCs that have faster processors.

FIND IT ON THE CD
TodayX, $3.99
MTUX
www.mtux.com

101 DVD-to-Pocket PC

Hey, Is That a DVD on Your Pocket PC?

Can we get philosophical for a second? If you purchase a movie on DVD, it stands to reason you should be able to watch that movie wherever and however you like, right? We think so, too. That's why we're excited by DVD-to-Pocket PC, a simple program that converts DVD movies for viewing on your handheld.

Now for the caveat. Although the program can be purchased online from Handango (www.handango.com), there's a disclaimer saying it shouldn't be used by U.S. customers because of "regulatory limitations." In other words, in this country you're not supposed to rip movies from DVDs, even though it's legal to rip songs from CDs. Go figure.

Assuming you're willing to "risk" using the software (we don't think Hollywood thugs—by which we mean lawyers—are going to break down your door), you'll find it ideal for copying DVDs to your Pocket PC. Actually, "ideal" may be too strong a word. In a couple of the movies we converted, the audio was slightly out of sync with the video. They were watchable, but a bit frustrating at the same time.

One more caveat: DVD-to-Pocket PC encodes movies in the Windows Media Player 9 format, meaning your PDA must have the Windows Mobile 2003 operating system. The movie files will not play on Pocket PC 2002 devices.

To use DVD-to-Pocket PC, you need a DVD-ROM drive (or DVD burner) installed in or connected to your PC. Insert the movie you want to copy, click Open, and then select the title from the list that appears. Don't know which one to choose? The actual movie is invariably the title with the longest length. Click OK, and in a moment you should see the DVD menu appear in the onscreen Pocket PC. Next, choose a quality setting for your movie: Normal or High. The former will fit a 100-minute movie onto a 128MB memory card, while the latter requires a 256MB-or-larger card.

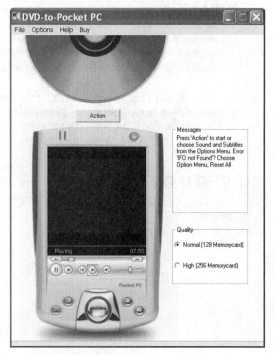

Once you've made your selection, click Action—and then go see a movie. It'll take a few hours for DVD-to-Pocket PC to copy the DVD and encode it for viewing on your PDA. When it's done, you'll end up with a file called DVD.wmv on your Windows desktop. Rename it as desired (Nemo.wmv or whatever—just make sure to keep the .wmv extension), then copy it to your memory card. Fire up Windows Media Player on your Pocket PC, and you're ready for the popcorn.

Killer Tip   *Want to save yourself $25? There are ways to rip movies from DVDs and convert them for Pocket PC viewing without DVD-to-Pocket PC—but none as easy and automated. Still, if you're highly tech-savvy and want to explore the options, start at DVDRhelp.com, where you'll find information on ripping DVDs and encoding the files in Pocket PC format.*

FIND IT ON THE CD
DVD-to-Pocket PC, $24.99
Makayama Software
www.omegaone.com

Appendix

About the CD

The CD that comes with *101 Killer Apps for Your Pocket PC* contains:

- Trial versions or shareware of a selection of the tools discussed in the book for you to try out

- Live links to the web sites where you can access the latest versions of all 101 Killer Apps covered in the book

We have included applications for download from those manufacturers who provided us with a written, signed agreement to include their applications on the CD. The applications discussed in the book—from 1 to 101—are all listed with their corresponding links to the latest version of each tool. Please note that the link on the CD was the latest version at the time the book and CD went to press.

Any tool listed on the CD that has a CD icon in the far left-hand column next to the tool name is available for download directly from the CD. Many of these tools are trial or demo versions that time-out after a certain period. For the latest version of the applications discussed in the book, you can use the URL next to each of the tools listed on the CD to access the manufacturers' web sites.

How to Use the CD-ROM

After you launch the CD, you will need to agree to the terms in the End User License Agreement. Once you agree, you will see the GNU Public License. After reading this, click the OK button. Clicking the authors' names will take you to a page with more information about the lead authors.

In the center of the cover there is a Link To 101 Apps button that will take you to the applications on the CD and to the links to all 101 Killer Apps discussed in the book. To the left of the cover, you will find bookmarks, which you can use to navigate to the different components on the CD. There, you will find information on how to use the CD and Adobe Acrobat Reader.

Applications on the CD

The Link To 101 Apps page includes all 101 Killer Apps discussed in the book, along with the latest URL for each tool, in case you need more information on how to install the tool or want to download the most recent version online. When you click the application name, you may see a dialog box that reads:

"The file D:\OPENE~14.EXE is set to be launched by this PDF file. The file may contain programs, macros, or viruses that could potentially harm your computer. Only open the file if you are sure it is safe. If this file was placed by a trusted person or program then click Open to view this file."

Click the box that reads Do Not Show This Message Again, and click the Open button. Then, Acrobat will take you to the folder where all of the tools are located. There you will find folders for each tool. Double-click the tool you want to access, and then you will see the actual tool file ready for you to install on your system.

The table that follows lists the 101 Killer Apps included in the book. Applications with a CD icon are included on the CD.

NOTE   *The links contained on the CD are the latest links available at the time this book went to press.*

	Killer App	Price	Company	URL
	1. Textmaker	$49.95	SoftMaker Software	www.softmaker.de
	2. Presenter-to-Go	$199	MARGI Systems	www.margi.com
●	3. Pocket SlideShow	$19.95	CNetX	www.cnetx.com
	4. Minutes of Meeting	$6.99	Dreamee Soft	www.dreameesoft.com
	5. PocketPrint	$39.95	Anycom	www.anycom.com
	6. IA ScreenShot	$9.95	IA Style	www.iastyle.com
	7. PI*Today*	$10	DeJe Online	www.pitoday.de.vu
	8. Pocket Outliner	$12.99	DSRTech	www.dsrtech.net
●	9. powerOne Finance	$59.99	Infinity Softworks	www.infinitysw.com
	10. MobileDB	$29.99	Handmark	www.handmark.com
●	11. RepliGo	$29.95	Cerience	www.cerience.com
●	12. PocketPrivacy	$24.95	PocketMind	www.pocketmind.com
	13. myCard	$4.95	Pedro Ivo Faria	www.handango.com
	14. Vingido	$24.95 annual subscription	Vindigo	www.vindigo.com
	15. HandMap	$16 plus maps	HandMap	www.handmap.net
●	16. Zagat To Go 2004	$24.95 (CD or download, one-year subscription)	Zagat	www.zagat.com
●	17. Voice Translator Multilingual Edition	$40	Speereo	www.speereo.com
	18. Pocket Travel Dictionary	$9.99	AIM Productions	www.aimproductions.be
●	19. TripTracker	$29.95	Two Peaks Solutions	www.twopeaks.com
	20. Mapopolis Navigator	Free (maps extra)	Mapopolis	www.mapopolis.com

Killer App	Price	Company	URL
21. Veo PhotoTraveler	$79.99 ($99 version for the Dell Axim available, as well)	Veo	www.veo.com
22. Flip It!	$4.99	Digital Concepts	www.dig-concepts.com
23. Pocket Artist	$49.95	Conduits Technologies	www.conduits.com
24. resco Picture Viewer	$19.95	resco	www.resco-net.com
25. Z4Music	$9	Z4Soft	www.z4soft.com
26. Pocket Chord Finder	$9.99	Rock Stevens Software	www.rockstevens.com
27. Microsoft Reader	Free	Microsoft	www.microsoft.com/reader
28. ReaderWorks Standard	Free	OverDrive	www.overdrive.com/ readerworks/
29. Total Remote	$24.99	Griffin Technology	www.griffintechnology.com
30. PocketTV	Free	Pocket TV	www.pockettv.com
31. Pocket Player	$19.95	Conduits Technologies	www.conduits.com
32. Replay Radio	$29.95	Applian	www.replay-radio.com
33. CEPlaylist	$9.95	Creative Engineering	www.ceng.com
34. Wine Enthusiast Guide	$19.95	LandWare	www.landware.com
35. BarBack Drink Guide	$9.95	Town Compass	www.pocketdirectory.com
36. MoviesCE	$19.95	Patrice Pennetier	www.pocketpc.pennetier.com
37. Pocket Stars	$19.95	Nomad Electronics	www.nomadelectronics.com
38. Personal Vehicle Manager	$19.95	Two Peaks Software	www.twopeaks.com
39. Diet & Exercise Assistant	$19.95	Keyoe, Inc	www.keyoe.com
40. IntelliGolf 7.0 Birdie Edition	$39.95	Karrier Communications	www.intelligolf.com
41. SimCity 2000	$29.95	Zio Interactive	www.ziointeractive.com
42. Merriam-Webster Crossword Challenge	$14.95	Hexacto	www.hexacto.com

	Killer App	Price	Company	URL
	43. The Emperor's Mahjong	$14.95	Hexacto	www.hexacto.com
●	44. Trivial Pursuit	$29.99	Handmark	www.handmark.com
●	45. Battleship, Scrabble, Yahtzee	Battleship, $19.99 Scrabble, $29.99 Yahtzee, $19.99	Handmark	www.handmark.com
●	46. All Mobile Casino	$14.95	BinaryFish	www.binaryfish.com
	47. ChessGenius	$25	Lang Software	www.chessgenius.com
●	48. Backgammon	$14.99	Handmark	www.handmark.com
	49. Billiard Master	$19.95	DigYs	www.digys.com
	50. Text Twist	$14.95	Astraware	www.astraware.com
●	51. PocketConquest	$20	Sean O'Connor's Windows Games	www.windowsgames.co.uk
	52. Chopper Alley	$19	Zio Interactive	www.ziointeractive.com
●	53. Darxide EMP	$7	Frontier Developments	www.frontier.co.uk
	54. PDA Playground	$19.95	DataViz	www.dataviz.com
●	55. Time Recorder	$15	Owlseeker Solutions	www.owlseeker.co.uk
●	56. Agenda Fusion	$29.95	DeveloperOne	www.developerone.com
●	57. ListPro	$19.95	Ilium Software	www.iliumsoft.com
●	58. BugMe!	$19.95	Electric Pocket	www.electricpocket.com
●	59. Decuma OnSpot	$29.95	Decuma	www.decuma.com
●	60. Tapless	$29.95	Synaptek Software	www.tapless.com
	61. VoiceGo!	$9.95	PDAWin	www.pdawin.com
●	62. NotesToday	$5	enVision	http://evs.dellama.com
	63. LoanTools	$24.95	PPC Software	www.handango.com
●	64. Unit Converter	Free	Maximilian Wimmer	www.handango.com

Killer App	Price	Company	URL
65. DateMate	$9.95	MobiMate	www.mobimate.com
66. visual Key	$15	sfr GmbH	www.viskey.de
67. Oxford American Desk Dictionary and Thesaurus	$29.99 (MMC version, $49.99)	Handmark	www.handmark.com
68. emAnalogy	$15.95	Encom Emsys Technologies	www.allmobileworld.com
69. 4.0Student	$29.99 (includes one year of Fourostudent.net)	Handmark	www.handmark.com
70. ePocrates Rx Pro	Free	ePocrates, Inc.	www.epocrates.com
71. The 2004 World Almanac, Handheld Edition Bundle	$11.95	Town Compass	www.pocketdirectory.com
72. FlashCards 101	$10.99	MyPocket Technologies	www.mypocket-technologies.com
73. Zaz Kids Alphabet (and other titles)	$1.99 each	Zaz	www.handango.com
74. AvantGo	Free	AvantGo	www.avantgo.com
75. VeriChat	$24.95, $19.95 annually after the first year	PDAapps	www.pdaapps.com
76. VITO VoiceDialer and VITO VoiceDialer PE	$15.95	VITO Technology	www.vitotechnology.com
77. ThunderHawk	$49.95 per year	Bitstream	www.bitstream.com
78. OneMail	$29.95	Brightex Technology Limited	http://net.worth.com .hk/onemail
79. riteMail	$29.95	Pen&Internet	www.ritemail.net
80. Simple SMS	$21	Visual IT	www.visualit.co.uk
81. BuZZone	$29.95	BuZZone	www.buzzone.net
82. Stock Manager	$24.95	TinyStocks	www.tinystocks.com
83. Mastersoft Money	$29.95	Mastersoft Mobile Solutions	www.mastersoftmobilesolutions .com

Killer App	Price	Company	URL
84. Rebate Information Tracker	Free	Binh Ho	www.handango.com
85. Financial Analyzer	$29.99	PocketSoftWear.com	www.pocketsoftwear.com
86. Car Loan Calculator	$4.95	Implicit Software Solutions	www.implicitsoftware.com
87. Journal Bar	$14.99	Omega One	www.omegaone.com
88. eXPerience	$19.99	Digital Expedition	www.digitalexpedition.com
89. Explorer 2003	$19.95	resco	www.resco-net.com
90. SuperCalendar	$9.95	ScaryBear Software	www.scarybearsoftware.com
91. Palm Reader	Free	Palm Digital Media	www.palmdigitalmedia.com
92. StartPad	$7.50	Stellarmetrics	www.stellarmetrics.com
93. Battery Pack	$19.99	Omega One	www.omegaone.com
94. PocketMusic	$19.95	PocketMind, Inc.	www.pocketmind.com
95. PocketPC Mark	$6.95	Anton Tomov	www.antontomov.com
96. Pocket Earth	$14.95	Blue Point Studio	www.bluepointstudio.com
97. GeoKron	$12.95	Vistasoft, Inc.	www.geokron.com
98. Remote Display Control for Pocket PC	Free	Microsoft	www.microsoft.com/ windowsmobile/resources/ downloads/pocketpc/ powertoys.mspx
99. Dose-A-Day	$19.95	DataViz	www.dataviz.com
100. TodayX	$3.99	MTUX	www.mtux.com
101. DVD-to-Pocket PC	$24.99	Makayama Software	www.omegaone.com

Getting Started

The CD-ROM is optimized to run under Windows 95/98/NT/ME/2000/2003/XP/ Server 2003 using the Adobe Acrobat Reader version 5.0 included on the disc. To install the tools on your computer, insert the CD into your CD disc drive. In most cases, a setup program will start automatically. (It may take a few moments for the opening windows to appear on your screen. If the indicator light is flashing on your CD drive, the program is still loading.)

Windows 95/98/NT/ME/2000/2003/XP/ Server 2003

The CD will start automatically when you insert the CD in the drive. If the program does not start automatically, your system may not be set up to detect CDs automatically. You can start the program by double-clicking the My Computer icon on the Windows desktop. When the My Computer window opens, double-click the icon for your CD drive. The program should start. If it doesn't, you should now see a list of the CD's contents. Look for the file named start or start.exe. Double-click this file to start the program.

If you prefer, you can run the contents of the CD from your hard drive without having to use the CD. To do so, right-click the CD drive, select Open, copy the book folder to your hard drive, and install the version of Adobe Acrobat Reader supported by your operating system (see the instructions below). Once this is done, you can start the program by opening the book folder and double-clicking the file named cover or cover.pdf. This will automatically start the associated Acrobat Reader. For convenience, you can create a shortcut to the cover file and place it on your desktop. You will then be able to start the program by clicking the shortcut.

To install Acrobat Reader, double-click the My Computer icon on your desktop. When the My Computer window opens, double-click the icon for your CD drive. You should now see a list of the contents of the CD. Double-click the folder named Install. Within this folder, double-click the subfolder that corresponds to your version of the Windows operating system. In this folder, you will see a file named ar505enu or ar505enu.exe. Double-click this file to start the installation program. Alternatively, the most up-to-date version of Adobe Acrobat Reader is available for free download at www.adobe.com.

Windows 3.1

For Windows 3.1 users, you must use Acrobat Reader version 3.0, which is included on the CD. You must install the program on your hard drive. To install it, copy the book folder to your hard drive, and then install Acrobat Reader 3.0 for Windows. Then, to run the program, open the book folder and double-click the cover.pdf file.

Macintosh

For the CD to start automatically, you must be running under Mac OS version 8.6–9 (Autorun is not supported on Macintosh OS X). The title page should automatically display within a minute of inserting the CD. If the CD does not launch, you can start the program manually by double-clicking the CD-ROM icon on your desktop and then double-clicking the Start icon.

If you prefer, you can run the program from your hard drive without having to use the CD. To do so, copy the files to your hard drive and install Acrobat Reader.

Note *You must do this if you are using a 68K Macintosh.*

Unix

Go to www.adobe.com to locate Adobe Acrobat Reader for the following operating systems:

- Linux
- IBM AIX
- Sun OS
- SGI IRIX
- Sun Solaris
- HP-UX
- DEC OSF/1

To install the program, copy the book directory to your hard drive. Then install the appropriate version of Adobe Acrobat Reader. You may then start the program from your hard drive.

Problems with the CD

If you have followed the instructions above, and the program will not work, you may have a defective drive or a defective CD. Be sure the CD is inserted properly in the drive. (Test the drive with other CDs to see if they run.)

If you live in the U.S. and the CD included in your book has defects in materials or workmanship, please call McGraw-Hill at 1-800-217-0059, 9 A.M. to 5 P.M. (EST), Monday through Friday, and McGraw-Hill will replace the defective disc. If you live outside the U.S., please contact your local McGraw-Hill office. You can find contact information for most offices on the International Contact Information page immediately following the index of this book, or send an e-mail to omg_international@mcgraw-hill.com.

Index

Numbers

4.0Student application, features of, 133–135
2004 World Almanac Handheld Edition bundle, features of, 137–138

A

ADD (American Desk Dictionary), features of, 130–131
Adobe Acrobat files, manipulating with RepliGo, 20–22
Agenda Fusion application, features of, 108–110
AIM Productions, web address for, 35
alarms
    setting with BugMe!, 112–113
    setting with GeoKron, 192
All Mobile Casino game, features of, 92–94
almanac, The 2004 World Almanac Handheld Edition bundle, features of, 137–138
alphabet application, Zaz Kids, 140–142
amortization tables, generating with LoanTools application, 122
analogy application, features of, 132–133
Animated Today program, web address for, 197
animations, creating with Flip It!, 43–44
annuity worksheets, availability in Financial Analyzer, 169
Anthelion outer-space game, web address for, 101
Anycom, web address for, 10
Applian's Replay Radio, web address for, 64, 66
applications, finding, 117
Astraware's Text Twist game, web address for, 98
astronomy resource, Pocket Stars as, 73–76
AvantGo application
    features of, 146–148
    vs. Journal Bar, 174

B

Backgammon game, features of, 95–96
backups, making, 39
BarBack Drink Guide, features of, 70–71
battery life, improving, 143
Battery Pack application, features of, 183–184
Battleship game, features of, 90–91
benchmarks, performing with PocketPC Mark, 188
Billiard Master game, features of, 96–97
BinaryFish's All Mobile Casino game, web address for, 94
Binh Ho's Rebate Information Tracker, web address for, 169
Birdie Edition of IntelliGolf, features of, 82–83
Bitstream's ThunderHawk, web address for, 153
Blue Point Studio's Pocket Earth application, web address for, 191
Bluetooth, 38
    advisory about, 9
    pairing devices for use of, 162

uses for, 158
using BuZZone with, 160–162
using Simple SMS with, 157–160
using with VITO VoiceDialer, 150–151
books. *See* e-books
Brightex Technology Limited's OneMail, web address for, 155
Brother printers, features of, 10
browser, ThunderHawk, 152–153
BugMe! application, hypercharging notes with, 112–113
business cards, creating and managing with MyCard, 24–26
business math, performing with powerOne Finance, 17
business presentations, creating with Presenter-to-Go, 4–5
BuZZone application, features of, 160–162

C

calculator, using powerOne Finance as, 16–18
calendar applications
    Dose-A-Day, 194–196
    SuperCalendar, 179–180
Calendar calculations, performing with powerOne Finance, 17
Calendar feature, supercharging with Agenda Fusion, 108–110
Calendar Plus Today, web address for, 180
cameras. *See* digital cameras
Canon printers, features of, 10
card sets, building for FlashCards 101, 139
car leasing worksheets, availability in Financial Analyzer, 169
Car Loan Calculator application, features of, 171–172
cars, tracking maintenance of, 76–78
cash flow worksheets, availability in Financial Analyzer, 169
casino game, All Mobile Casino, 92–94
CEPlaylist, managing MP3 collections with, 66–67
Cerience's RepliGo, web address for, 22
channels, setting up for AvantGo, 146–147
chat applications, VeriChat, 148–149
ChessGenius game, features of, 94–95
children's books, downloading, 142
Chopper Alley game, features of, 99–101
chords, finding with Pocket Chord Finder, 50–51
cities
    calculating distances between, 192
    managing with SimCity 2000 game, 84–85
clock application, GeoKron, 191–192
Close to Home calendar, availability in Dose-A-Day, 194–196
CNetX's Pocket SlideShow, web address for, 7
Conduits Technologies
    Pocket Artist, 46
    Pocket Player, 64

INTERNATIONAL CONTACT INFORMATION

AUSTRALIA
McGraw-Hill Book Company
Australia Pty. Ltd.
TEL +61-2-9900-1800
FAX +61-2-9878-8881
http://www.mcgraw-hill.com.au
books-it_sydney@mcgraw-hill.com

CANADA
McGraw-Hill Ryerson Ltd.
TEL +905-430-5000
FAX +905-430-5020
http://www.mcgraw-hill.ca

**GREECE, MIDDLE EAST, & AFRICA
(Excluding South Africa)**
McGraw-Hill Hellas
TEL +30-210-6560-990
TEL +30-210-6560-993
TEL +30-210-6560-994
FAX +30-210-6545-525

MEXICO (Also serving Latin America)
McGraw-Hill Interamericana Editores
S.A. de C.V.
TEL +525-1500-5108
FAX +525-117-1589
http://www.mcgraw-hill.com.mx
carlos_ruiz@mcgraw-hill.com

SINGAPORE (Serving Asia)
McGraw-Hill Book Company
TEL +65-6863-1580
FAX +65-6862-3354
http://www.mcgraw-hill.com.sg
mghasia@mcgraw-hill.com

SOUTH AFRICA
McGraw-Hill South Africa
TEL +27-11-622-7512
FAX +27-11-622-9045
robyn_swanepoel@mcgraw-hill.com

SPAIN
McGraw-Hill/
Interamericana de España, S.A.U.
TEL +34-91-180-3000
FAX +34-91-372-8513
http://www.mcgraw-hill.es
professional@mcgraw-hill.es

**UNITED KINGDOM, NORTHERN,
EASTERN, & CENTRAL EUROPE**
McGraw-Hill Education Europe
TEL +44-1-628-502500
FAX +44-1-628-770224
http://www.mcgraw-hill.co.uk
emea_queries@mcgraw-hill.com

ALL OTHER INQUIRIES Contact:
McGraw-Hill/Osborne
TEL +1-510-420-7700
FAX +1-510-420-7703
http://www.osborne.com
omg_international@mcgraw-hill.com